IBCZ2796

The Mother Town

Map of Scotland and the Borders.

THE
MOTHER
TOWN

Civic Ritual, Symbol,
and Experience
in the Borders of Scotland

Gwen Kennedy Neville

New York   Oxford
OXFORD UNIVERSITY PRESS
1994

Oxford University Press

Oxford   New York   Toronto
Delhi   Bombay   Calcutta   Madras   Karachi
Kuala Lumpur   Singapore   Hong Kong   Tokyo
Nairobi   Dar es Salaam   Cape Town
Melbourne   Auckland   Madrid

and associated companies in
Berlin   Ibadan

Copyright © 1994 by Gwen Kennedy Neville

Published by Oxford University Press, Inc.
200 Madison Avenue, New York, New York 10016

Oxford is a registered trademark of Oxford University Press, Inc.

Library of Congress Cataloging-in-Publication Data
Neville, Gwen Kennedy, 1938–
The mother town : civic ritual, symbol, and experience in
the borders of Scotland /
Gwen Kennedy Neville.
p.   cm.   Includes bibliographical references and index.
ISBN 0-19-508837-9   ISBN 0-19-509032-2 (pbk)
1. Borders Region (Scotland)—Social life and customs.
2. Rites and ceremonies—Scotland—Borders Region.
3. City and town life—Scotland—Borders Region.
4. Symbolism—Scotland—Borders Region.
I. Title.   DA880.B72N48   1994
941.1—dc20   93-6062

2 4 6 8 9 7 5 3 1

Printed in the United States of America
on acid-free paper

Preface

The idea of the individual as a separate and worthwhile person before God is a critical idea in Western European Protestant culture and
its colonial daughter cultures, especially in the Calvinist ideology of
the Church of Scotland and the Scottish Presbyterians abroad. It is
an idea not unconnected to that of capitalism and modernization—
as Weber and his followers have pointed out—an idea that fits neatly
with the imperative to fulfill one's "calling" or "potential," to "make
a life for oneself," to "seek one's fortune," requiring the congruent
notion of being willing to leave home. A second idea that holds prominence in this same religious–cultural world of thought and action—
and one that seems to contradict the first—is the idea of the community, home, loyalty to and membership in a corporate body, a group
that is transindividual and transgenerational. These two contradictory ideas play in and through the Protestant, capitalistic experience
and find periodic resolution only temporarily in certain literary and
ritual forms. For the wandering individual on the outward life journey of the Protestant pilgrim, one possible ritual symbolic construction of a reconciled person and group comes in the return journey to
reunions, homecomings, and other kin-religious gatherings of Scots
around the world. In these assemblies the group is reconstituted
symbolically in the regathering of kin and cobelievers around themes
of family, church, and town. In Scotland, cultural performances re-
create themes of clan, kirk, and burgh in the various regions and along

various lines of local history and experience. In the Borders region, this ritual reconciliation takes the shape and dramatic form of civic ceremonies known as *common ridings*. This book focuses on one such civic ritual in one ancient Border town as an instance of this ritual process—a drama enacting the conflicting demands for individuality and community—in other towns in other places throughout the Protestantized, modernized, postcolonial world.

The Background of This Study: Theory, Method, and Fieldwork

My search for solutions to the puzzles of cultural construction has led through an anthropological world of shifting paradigms. At the outset of this book I am faced with the task of positioning—or "siting" and "situating"—in, among, and in relation to the various available meaning systems of the scholarly scene in order to inform my reader of some of the background to my work. One traditional way of doing this in ethnographic writing is the long-standing convention of the Preface. In the Preface, the ethnographer reveals to the reader something of the process of the making of the book in both theory and method. This segment of an ethnographic work is a kind of behind-the-scenes peek at the book about to be unveiled, its positioning vis-à-vis the writer's life, its historical context, its theoretical underpinnings, and its proposed significance as seen by the author as it fits in with other works of other authors in the field of ethnology. The preface of an ethnographic study sometimes resembles the kind of television documentary that details the making of a particular film. Here, in my Preface, I have looked behind the scenes at my own theory and method as I locate this study among the array of other works, meanings, and truths we know as cultural anthropology.

The Process of Theory Making

I first visited Scotland in 1972 as a part of my long-term interest and study of what I then called the "cultural persistence" of British and European worlds in the southeastern United States. I was searching for the cultural antecedents of the family and church gatherings in the American South—reunions, homecomings, camp meetings, cemetery association days. My original trip was a survey of Scottish regions and their most typical kinds of gatherings. It was on that first trip that I discovered the Borders and their common ridings.[1]

At first when I began to ask the questions attendant to discovering how cultures work and how they mean, I was operating out of a model from structural–functional anthropology delivered to me by Solon Kimball, Conrad Arensberg, and other teachers. This basic model was enriched by Kimball's own understandings and appreciation of ritual processes and the power of symbolization, especially symbolization in social scenes and performances, in the symbolic use of space, and in the design of human settlements. The assortment of ideas I had made my own had been gleaned from those of a wide variety of anthropologists and anthropological positions, an eclectic collection including notions from archaeology, linguistics, applied anthropology, and primate studies (especially ethology), all vying for conquest of my often unyielding underlayer of intellectual training as an undergraduate and beginning graduate in the field of English literature. In those days, it was difficult to fit all these competing themes and viewpoints into a way of thinking and researching a problem.

"Symbolic anthropology" as a term had not yet been invented when I entered graduate study in the mid-1960s, although it had certainly begun to be explored by the followers of Durkheim, Van Gennep, and W. Lloyd Warner. Gradually, those who were timidly finding their way—the less timid voices coming from Chicago and Harvard, later from Duke, Princeton, and Chapel Hill—read one another's articles and books and talked to one another at meetings. Over time, Geertz, Turner, and Schneider and their students, along with students of Kimball and Arensberg and other like-minded readers and writers, began to invent symbolic anthropology and reinvent cultural anthropology in various voices.[2]

Not only had "symbolic anthropology" not gained currency in the 1960s, but Europe and America had not gained respectability as locations for "real" anthropological fieldwork. One of the most important lessons I learned from Kimball and his copioneer Conrad Arensberg over the years was that research in American and British cultures had validity, that as students of human cultures and societies we should not fail to take seriously the significant cultural milieus in which we live as English speakers. I also gained an appreciation for the importance of solving the riddles of conflict, politics, economics, and social organization in our own cultural setting as well as in those of what was then known as the "primitive world." The power of culture in shaping the form of human settlements and giving shape to human social arrangements was a kind of baseline belief with which I approached my own problem or question, or set of problems and questions—the questions of the expression and continuity of culture over long periods of time among widely scattered populations of formerly contiguous culture bearers. The sociologists had pondered this puzzle throughout the late nineteenth century, framing their questions in terms of the dichotomy of gemeinschaft and gesellschaft, "traditional" and "modern," and "mechanical" versus "organic" solidarity as they watched the countrysides of France, Germany, and England rearranged through enclosures and industrial lure and as they tried to explain the ways in which humans had aligned themselves in the new towns and cities of the manufacturing and commercial world. Anthropologists had been slower to begin questioning the processes of modernization because they had been concentrating on the most remote peoples and communities they could find for their studies. Urban anthropology, like symbolic anthropology, was being invented within archaeology and social anthropology and often, like other new subfields, taking a seat on the sidelines to more traditionally established ways of studying culture. By the early 1970s, urban anthropology, like its other sisters in the study of complex societies, had taken its place in a respectable position, and today it cuts across the fields along with the cross-cutting, ready acceptance of European and American worlds as suitable locations for the study of culture.

Scotland emerged as an important image prefiguring the construction of the past for the community I studied in 1970 for my doctoral dissertation. This was the summer conference center at Montreat, North Carolina, of the then Southern Presbyterians, a denomination claiming descent primarily from the Scots and Scots–Irish immigrants to the southeastern United States. In the periodic gathering together of these scattered people, who were related through kinship, friendship, and coparticipation in summertime religious ceremonial life, I found one answer to my query of how culture can be constructed and maintained in an urban society. The answer here was that reassemblies for ritual processes enable the calling out of the full, or at least more full than usual, inventory of cultural materials and the arrangement of these into sequences of action that served as elaborate annual performances of significant cultural themes and narratives. In the summer community of Montreat I found a four-month long performance in which symbols of being Presbyterian were called forth and ceremonially manipulated so that in the end, generation after generation of families retained and passed along their cultural heritage (Neville 1974). Following the summer of 1970 and the production of my doctoral thesis, I began to explore additional examples of this regathering process, a complex I finally began to know as a Protestant pilgrimage (Neville 1987a).

The themes that continued to demand my attention in the Montreat community and in the family reunions, church homecomings, camp meetings, and cemetery associations I later studied included the themes of ancestry, especially ancestry from Scotland; kin group membership, especially all the descendants of one common ancestor; the idea of a Covenant community, a "chosen people"; and other Reformation motifs that tied these celebrants of Presbyterian American "ethnicity" to their transgenerational past in Ulster and the Scottish Lowlands. What began as a series of questions framed within a discourse on cultural continuity and the inquiry into "persistence" became rephrased over the years as questions of the symbolic construction of community, the processes of ritual expression, and eventually as questions of the overall pattern of the Protestant symbolic world in which conflicting demands exist and cannot be met, especially the contradictory demands to leave home and seek one's fortune and at the same time to stay at home to create a safe and secure covenant community.

As time went on, my focus on one community or one ritual of reunion at a time widened so that within my range of vision I could encompass larger historical and economic processes and understand some of the puzzling contradictions in the meanings that I was finding as I went forward in my inquiries. Throughout the 1970s my reading and collegial discussions began to take in the growing body of work in symbolic anthropology.[3] In the 1980s I added readings outward, including the work of the social and economic historians and those doing comparative and critical works in literature and anthropology, such as Eric Hobsbawn (1983), Marshall Sahlins (1976), Christopher Smout (1969, 1986), Raymond Williams (1973), and Eric Wolf (1982). And now on these are layered the complex and often troubling constructs and deconstructs of the postmodernists, and the annual assembled voices of the Society for Cultural Anthropology.

In 1979 I moved to Texas. My positioning shifted from the Southeast, where Atlanta and Emory University had been my fieldwork and teaching base, to the edge of the Scots–Irish frontier, where I found in Texas a widening field for ethnographic and literary endeavor. Over the years since 1979 a series of conversations with colleagues visiting the campus at Southwestern University as part of the annual Brown Symposium have become a part of my ever-shifting perspective. Clifford Geertz, James Boon, David Tracy, Stephen Greenblatt,

Roger Abrahams, James Peacock, Barbara Myerhoff, Dell Hymes, Annette Weiner, Sherry Ortner, and Michael Herzfeld have brought various social and cultural observations into my ken; William H. MacNeill, historical ones; and Kenneth Boulding, economic ones. In the musicology field I have gained new angles from symposia on Gustav Mahler and Benjamin Britten and from Thai music and performances of the Ramakien. These exposures to literary criticism and the critical analysis of performed art have made an indelible mark on my style of understanding, analyzing, and writing about my Scotland materials.[4] Ethnographic study on the Bible Belt Catholic project and conversations with colleagues Jon Anderson, Sam Hill, and others added further insights.

Meanwhile, the years since my first trip to Scotland held other return journeys, punctuated by the rethinking of field notes that changing theoretical perspectives invariably bring. The interplay of theories (models) with practice (methods) is one of the important distinguishing features of ethnography and the ethnological point of view. These methodological interplays deserve a separate discussion.

The Process of Ethnography

The fieldwork for this study began in the summer of 1972 and has continued through five periods of residence from that time to the present. Over the years I have collected histories of lives and towns; consulted ancient burgh records and the writings of local historians; interviewed the elderly and the young and the key participants in ceremonial life; taken walks on the hills with my friends; chatted with the butcher, baker, and greengrocer; ordered coal and lighted coal fires in the evenings; and cooked food and washed clothes much as did the other residents of Selkirk and much as other ethnographers have done in other settings. My husband began research in 1975 on aspects of Border life, especially on the ceremonial men's associations of the common ridings, as material for his own doctoral research in cultural anthropology. We lived on our various grants and fellowships over the various summers at the edge of the town in an old shepherd's cottage on an old farm.

Shawmount Farm, and Greenhead Farm adjoining, belonged to a family whom I came to know very well. The house at Shawmount— in whose "cottage" we lived—was occupied over a period of years by the shepherd's family, and the shepherd's wife became my valued neighbor and has remained my friend. One of my most treasured assistants was the town librarian, now deceased, who was one of my first acquaintances in Selkirk and whose advice, introductions, knowledge of the local scene, and kindly good humor have continued to be invaluable to me in my Scotland study. His wife has been an important friend to me, and I have shared with her my own pain and joy over children and parents and watched as her son grew to manhood and married to settle down in the town. My own children were present from time to time in the fieldwork, and they became my research assistants, as they had done in their younger childhood in my original fieldwork in North Carolina. In Scotland they played with the children of the farmer and the shepherd, gathered vegetables and watched the sheepshearing, and attended the local school for a time after their own school in the states went on summer vacation. My daughter Mary Grace later returned during her college years to visit again as a guest of her close friend of the Shawmount Farm days.

The rhythms of leaving and return became a part of our life and research. As the summers ended and the demands of university teaching called, we would pack up and return to the United States, spend the winter pondering, reading, and rearranging collected texts, and then on some future summer go back to Selkirk for more daily-life experiences and more intense ritual celebrations. It was our goal to attend and attempt to understand something of each of the Border common ridings, and so an important component of our method was to take part each weekend in whatever celebration was going on in whatever town was holding one. I was especially interested in detailing the differences among the festivals' structure, process, and symbols. It was also one of my interests to identify the role of the returning "exiles" or "colonials," because my own particular problem was to connect these reunion-type regatherings with other kinds of reunions I had been studying in the United States. It was also my concern to figure out some of the ways that the visible symbols of civic identity and the cycles of celebration and festivity fit with modern Protestant and traditional Roman Catholic views of reality.

The specific techniques of "collecting" that accompany the study of ritual and ceremony are familiar to those who have tried to document celebrations of all kinds. These include careful observation and record in one's notebook of the order of action of events, participants, costumes and other paraphernalia, use of space and of time, forms of assembly (as in the "dinner," "concert," or public ceremonial enactment), and forms of performance and display (as in the processional, parade, or casting of flags and laying of wreaths). Music is important and must be noted in the listening, singing, gathering of scores and texts, and tape-recording of as much singing as possible. Food is important as well, and as one eats and drinks one's way through a festival it becomes rather like an initiation rite of its own for the flagging ethnographer unaccustomed to the richness of such occasions. Photography is one of the best and most satisfying ways of saving the event for future study; color slides become a means of not only recreating the event but also teaching about it and eliciting from one's students observations one might have not noted. Now, in fact, filmmakers have come to the Borders to capture the rich visual imagery of the town festivals and ridings and have produced several documentaries for the BBC, as well as a videocassette for sale by a private marketer. All of the technology available, however, is, in my view, inferior to the experience of marching and singing in High Street or later sitting around the fireside listening to common riding lore, reminiscing over past ridings and past events, hearing about the tales of danger and near misses, and assembling one's own collection of experiences to tell at anthropological firesides in future times.

In presenting the material I have selected for telling in this book, I have sometimes moved between what scholars would identify as "levels of discourse." I tell of the scenes of the performance of common riding; I elaborate on the symbols of which they are composed; I describe the social and historical context and the lived experience of the people of the town; I bring in references to the work of other anthropologists and students of religion and society; and I quote from my own fieldnotes, which include the voices of Selkirk residents and voices of my own interpretation as fieldworker. The result is a mixed medium, a kind of ethnological collage, a use of all possible kinds of texts and voices as a way of communicating to the reader some of the embedded mystery and meaning of the ritual itself.

My early work and writing on Scotland was directed primarily toward exploring the assemblies of the *kirk* (which I treat as "outdoor ritual" and "folk liturgies") and discerning how these expressed cultural themes are coterminous with certain forms of community and then comparing these forms with those of the clan and the burgh. Over time I have come to see these forms as expressive of three threads running through Scottish and Scots–American cultural worlds—threads of family, church, and town. I have published an analysis of ritual gatherings in American Protestant culture that create a kin-religious symbolic universe among people who have left their homes to wander. I now turn my attention to the town as the cultural form for those who stayed home—a cultural form, I believe, that makes staying and leaving possible to choose and so becomes a crucial element in the construction of the modern world.

Acknowledgments

A number of persons and agencies have assisted as this work developed and progressed through the years. The agencies include the National Endowment for the Humanities Summer Stipend Program for 1976 and 1989; the Emory University Research Council; the Candler School of Theology; and the Brown Foundation, Inc., of Houston, Texas, through the endowment of the Elizabeth Root Paden Chair, which I have held since 1979 at Southwestern University. I am grateful to Emory colleagues Lore Metzger, Carole Hahn, Do Skypek, Betty Edwards, and Margaret Drummond for their support and assistance in the early days of the Scotland project; in more recent years, to those in the Writers' Group at Southwestern University for their always careful reading and discerning comments and to Farley Snell for insight and encouragement. I also wish to thank my colleagues in anthropology and European studies around the United States who have read and commented on papers and articles from this material as discussants at conferences or as editors and reviewers for journals and granting agencies. They include Jon Anderson, Ellen Badone, James Boon, Phyllis Chock, Jill Dubisch, Pamela Frese, Eugene Irschick, David Kertzer, Gail Kligman, James Peacock, Larry Taylor, and Herve Varenne.

In Scotland, I have been assisted in numerous ways by Christopher Smout of St. Andrews University and by Mary Noble, Emily Lyle, Margaret MacKay, and Hamish Henderson of the University of Edinburgh. Finally, and with the deepest gratitude, I thank my friends in the Borders, who have continuously extended to me and my family their hospitality, patience, and kindness and who have included us in common riding celebrations and in their hearts and lives. Jim and Nan Smith, Ian and Elsie MacDonald, Ethel and Terry Fairbairn, Grace Wilson, Janet MacKenzie, Stewart Roberts, Jack Harper, Walter Elliot, Eddie Douglas, Margaret and Kenneth Anderson, and Audrey and Jim Maxwell all have submitted to repeated queries and seemingly interminable attempts on my part to "get it right" as we returned year after year in the role of the "exiles" to Selkirk and the Borders.

For assistance during the preparation and production of the manuscript, I thank Dotty Secor, Kathy Buchhorn, Dan Yoxall, and the editors at Oxford University Press. And as always, I thank my now-adult children Katherine, Mary Grace, and Ken for all they have done.

The fieldwork on which this book is based was conducted in cooperation with my husband, Jack G. Hunnicutt, whose work on common ridings complements my own. Our works and lives have been influenced by each other's in ways that are difficult to untangle and assign. It is therefore with appreciation for his keen observation, attention to detail, encyclopedic recall of information, piercing analysis, and critical commentary that I dedicate this book to Jack, who loves Selkirk, common ridings, and, most of all, the play of ideas in cultural analysis.

Georgetown, Texas   G. K. N.
August 1993

Contents

The Mother Town

Introduction

In the vast moorland known as the Borders of Scotland, the ancient towns, or *burghs*, are sentinels of civic order amid an otherwise sparsely populated expanse of heath and meadow dominated by hills and Cheviot sheep. The stately towns form commercial islands linked together in patterns of trade in goods, in the exchange of people through marriage, and, in a very important way, in ceremonial performances. Each town, on a recurrent Friday or Saturday in summer, holds its own particular town ceremony or festival, and the other towns send representatives who are principal players in their own earlier or anticipated local performances. Hawick, Selkirk, Melrose, Peebles, Kelso, Jedburgh, Galashiels, Langholm, and Lauder each in turn call out their casts of riders and horses, foot processionals, silver bands, pipe bands, banners, emblems, costumes, vocal music, and actors in order to bring into being a dramatic statement about the burgh as a place and about other themes that run through the culture of Scottish Border life—themes of war and death, loss through emigration, the divisions within the town by trades and crafts, and the overarching theme of protecting the town against the "outside world" beyond the boundaries of its common land.

The generic term for the town festivals—one used in brochures from the tourist authority and by commentators from the BBC—is "common ridings." But this term is, in fact, a misnomer for most of the towns, for only a handful retain any ownership of their town's common lands, granted to them in medieval times when the towns were outposts of commercialism and national control. Four towns are said by the Borderers to have "real common ridings," that is, festivals that conform to the ideal of annually riding on horseback around the boundaries of the town's common lands in order to monitor the placement of the boundary markers, constantly in legendary danger of being moved by the "encroaching aristocracy."

The four "real" common ridings of Hawick, Selkirk, Langholm, and Lauder embody the full component of dramatic features focusing on the burgh ownership of the commons, the rights of the citizen, and the honor and loss of the town's young men in war and through emigration. All of the other town festivals include as one feature some "riding out" to various points on horseback in procession, but instead of having the riding of commons be the central feature, the main theme may be another element of civic life, with an appropriate label for the event. These elements include historic events, as in the granting of the town charter in the town of Galashiels, or a place, such as the local ruined abbey as in Melrose and Kelso, or, as in Peebles, a traditional fair day—in the Peebles case, one with pre-Christian themes, known as the Beltane Fair. Also known in the tourist literature simply as "town festivals," these civic celebrations march one by one through the summer months as separate but interconnected enactments, involving the marshaling of immense quantities of resources in the form of money, horses, costumes, ritual paraphernalia, food and drink, rented spaces for concerts, dinners, balls, and human actors whose energy and time are required to stage these elaborate events. The common ridings, or festivals, have a resounding impact on the people who participate in them, especially those who serve as "principals" leading the horse processions as a chosen town representative, carrying the flag, serving as an attendant to the representative of the town, riding in the cavalcade, serving as a standard bearer for an ancient guild to cast its flag, or serving as a holder of a banner or symbol in foot processionals. The shared aura of participation over the years creates ritual veterans in each town who have a commonality of experience that brings year after year an almost magical quality to the event in the present and in memory.

One feature of the common ridings is that goods and services are redistributed; people are moved about on the landscape; the town's identity is affirmed; and social cohesion is established and maintained. Beyond these fairly straightforward economic and social functions, however, rest deeper levels of cultural importance and creativity, beyond the questions of social organization and political economy. These additional levels find expression in the symbols and images called out for performance, arranged in sequences of drama and narrative to tell a story about the towns, a story that the townsfolk and their ancestors have been constructing over the centuries. In other words, the performance of one common riding in one town is very like an opera that is performed in a particular opera house on one day each year. It most certainly has significance as an economic and a social event. But in addition, the opera has been composed by someone at some time and place, and it includes in its fabric of words, music, and action a series of recurring symbolic statements that can be viewed on their own by the music critic and the educated literary public.

In my analysis of the Border common ridings, I use one town, Selkirk, and I look in elaborate detail at the Selkirk Common Riding. For me it conveys eloquently the classic message of the festivals and ridings of all the Border towns, serving here not so much as a "sample" in the sense of any scientific effort at selection but truly as a "sampler" in the sense that it is an example of goods or works.[1]

In any critical study of music or drama, one selects in this way an artistic production that represents in its structure, process, and symbol some of the basic themes and meanings of an "age" or a "trend" in artistic development. In this same way, I have selected Selkirk and its common riding to represent the age and range of creative possibilities found throughout the Borders and, on a larger stage, throughout the European cultural worlds. Often in my discussion of a feature or of a theme, I refer to elements in other towns, for some towns have elaborated one or another item into a fascinating display of a particular idea. But it is always Selkirk on which I train my lens and whose ceremony and whose people are at the heart of my understanding of the common riding mysteries.

I view the common riding as a spectacle of music and drama staged through the studied and dedicated work of a cast and a production team, calling on a particular inventory of cultural symbols and materials to tell a story that makes a statement about some of the underlying conflicts and contradictions in the drama of everyday life. This is not just about the "human condition" or the "universal human" but also about being a human in a specific time and place—in this case, in the Borders with its own unique culture and history. To understand the statement being made by an opera or a play—that is, to be an appreciative member of the audience—one must understand a certain amount about the cultural constructs within which it has been composed and performed. All great works of art are set within a time and space but comment, in addition, on another time and space, or on all times and places known to the humans in that culture.

The common riding as a cultural form is a work of performed art that is not recorded in librettos and musical scores but only in the memory of the generations of people who have created and recreated it in the streets of their town over the centuries. In this book I attempt to unravel some of the mysteries of the operalike spectacle of horses, people, and music as an art form composed by a culture, by groups and communities of people over time rather than by one composer sitting in a studio in a cottage or a windmill. Just as the operas of Verdi or of Britten comment on certain conflicts and themes of cultural human significance, so do the common ridings: on town membership, on belonging to the burgh and the pain of leaving; on the honor and glory of war countered by the grief of loss and loneliness; on the elegant partition of people into groups through guilds and organizations against the idealized egalitarianism of burgh citizenship; of the tie between the countryside and the burgh, two contradictory and contrastive social forms enmeshed in the absolute necessity for economic interdependence; of the separateness and proud isolation of burgh identity against the further necessity of participating in an interburgh network and in the larger network of a world system propelling the burghs down roads they cannot change or control.

And so it is with this viewpoint of the cultural "critic," the informed observer and discerner of symbols, that I undertake the task of documenting and, to the extent I am able, explaining the complex and beautiful cultural form of the Selkirk Common Riding.

The Design of the Book: Ritual, Symbol, and Experience

In this book I present the Selkirk Common Riding as an elaborate performance—a drama, a "street opera"—that has been composed by the people of a town. The common riding symbols and their structures and referents are one focal point in my analysis. As an evolving, developing art form, the common riding has been created over several centuries of invention and elaboration on the basic functional act of perambulating the boundaries of the town's common lands. Over the years, the ritual inspection of boundary stones by a small troop of town burgesses has become the center of the town's ceremonial and symbolic life. My second focal point is this process, an example of the way in which civic ritual takes on "enlarged importance" in the gradual construction and reconstruction of the meanings of "the town." Third, I emphasize the relation of the ceremony, in all its aesthetic and symbolic complexity, to the actual lived experience of the town's people. This involves the expression and the repeated re-creation of social arrangements and social organization in and through symbolic and ritual forms. It also involves the relation of symbolic life to everyday life and to the larger patterns of history. The Selkirk Common Riding, in other words, is seen here as an elaborate processual metaphor in song, story, and pageantry, a metaphor for the town itself.

My exploration is aimed in part at uncovering some of the ways that metaphor works and means. Each scene of the common riding contains a vast amount of information, some of which I will attempt to draw out and interpret through an ethnological lens. Key themes emerge as central overarching messages throughout the unfolding sequence. These themes have to do with, first, external boundaries, especially boundaries of the town against the "outside world"; second, internal boundaries of segmented groups whose roles and positions are closely tied to the traditional life of the town; and, third, with losses to the town of its young men through war, death, and emigration. It is these themes of boundaries and loss that play in and through common riding imagery and ultimately, I maintain, create the key symbol of the town as Mother and Home against images of "away" and "outside" in the ongoing war between tradition and modernization in which towns throughout the Western world have been engaged over a long period of history.

Why, one might ask, did I choose the Selkirk Common Riding for such a close reading? What about the other Border towns and their common ridings or festivals? And more pointedly, why would I presume that in this one small town in a marginal region of a nation marginal to Europe I might find a sample for understanding symbolic construction and social transformation as a general process?

The answers to these very reasonable queries must be given on several practical and intellectual planes. For a start, Selkirk provides a classic example of civic nationalism, that is, the making of the town in Europe as part of the empire building and later the building of nationalism through the establishment of a civic presence. Selkirk was created by one of Scotland's early Norman kings in the twelfth century as a royal burgh at the same time as the royal establishment of feudal domains and the creation of abbeys in the attempt at creating a centralized Scottish nation under the symbolic headship of the monarch. Second, Selkirk gives us an example of the process of civic ritual encoding civic identity, a process that is documented for early towns of the Roman Empire, towns in Renaissance Italy, and towns in France after the Revolution of 1789. Finally, Selkirk provides an example of a Protestant, capitalist town, daughter of a rational-technical world, in which, surprisingly, elaborate ritual remains very strong. Selkirk is situated in a region of Scotland, the Lowlands, where one does not expect to encounter elaborate ritual pageantry. The common riding, in fact, calls out strikingly Catholic symbols and social forms in a part of Europe where the sacred symbols, mysteries, and liturgies of Roman Catholicism were banned over four hundred years ago. And for all these reasons, the common riding ceremony cries out for explanation.

As for my selection of Selkirk as the site for long-term fieldwork over the other Border towns, there are a number of reasons here as well. I might have taken as my focus one of the other royal burghs in the Borders, each one having its own unique style of civic pageantry, or I might have taken one of the other four towns said to hold the "real common ridings," each of which has some of the characteristics of Selkirk's common riding. Over the years I have attended and carefully documented all four of these—Hawick, Selkirk, Langholm, and Lauder. I have attended each of the town festivals in the other Border burghs—Peebles, Melrose, Galashiels, Kelso, and Jedburgh—and assembled information on each through interviews, analyses of histories and brochures, and participation and ethnographic observation. Through the combination of careful choice and happy accident, I found Selkirk to be the town best suited to my residence and its common riding to be the most appropriate as my ethnographic window into civic ritual in the Borders. I find it to be a fitting instance of civic ritual in a wider, European context, as one process in the multiple and often competing symbolic transformations attending the long-term changes from a traditional and Catholic world to one of rationality, capitalism, and the Protestant construction of reality.

The Pattern of Theory and Themes

The theoretical framework within which this book is situated comes from symbolic anthropology, a kind of hybrid resulting from scholarly crosses between studies of symbols, religions, histories, and texts all directed at understanding cultures over time and space. This book has three main themes, presented in three parts.

Common Riding as Performance, Ritual, and Play

The focus of Part I is on the nature of ritual and symbols, especially civic symbols and rituals in relation to religious ones. The use of the image of the mother is significant here, in representing both church and town and also nation, as in mother country. This inquiry into the nature of symbols and their cultural workings is connected to the structure of culture and the definitions of persons and groups and also categories of classification. For instance, we find in the town ceremony a clear distinction between inside and outside, home and away, belonging to the town and being an incomer. We find strong imagery opposing the categories of Selkirk versus all the rest of the world (a variation on "ourselves" and "others" in which the in-group is confined to those born on the burgh soil). I believe that it is this symbolic boundary marking and the symbolic statement of the town as the mother—just as the church was formerly the mother of its people —that holds the key to answering the question of staying and leaving.

I believe also that the town as a social form stands between the closed corporate body of the medieval church and the open, movable world of individual possibilities that one finds in modern, mobile urban society. In the ideal world of the late twentieth century, one crosses boundaries and holds multiple group affiliations while at the same time carving out one's destiny alone. The individual person who has responded to the imperative to leave home is the protypical actor in a universe of mobility and individuality, in contrast with the protypical actor of a corporate, closed community such as the ancient church and village. It is my tentative hypothesis that both social categories (the "stayers" and the "leavers") can exist in the symbolic world of the town in the same semantic space and that the alternation between staying and leaving becomes a part of the fabric of meanings that is woven through ritual.

The Town in Symbol and Experience

The second theme, that of the town as a feature of Western culture, its symbolization of the civic, order, nationalism, and empire, is the focus of Part II. The representation of the town is also seen in relation to the representation of the church, especially the traditional medieval Roman Catholic church. I ask of each of these forms, "How in this particular way of thinking and seeing is the meaning of the *individual* defined in relation to the *corporate* body?" And I ask an additional question here, "What are the contributing images, symbols, and meanings that give rise to a world in which a person sees himself or herself in a new way, as a "detachable individual," as a person who can "leave?"

The Social Construction of "Meaning": Interpretations

The book's third theme appears as Part III, "The Interpretations." This section addresses questions about the social process of creating and continuing (producing and reproducing) ritual forms that at the same time represent past experience and shape experience, give it meaning, and set its direction for the future. The manipulation of symbols for political ends and the reassignment of symbols from one realm into another, that is, religious into civic, is a process that has engaged the attention of a number of anthropologists and other students of religion and society, from Durkheim to the present. This process is more than the "use" of symbols for materialist gains or the "invention of tradition" in the interest of the elite against that of the workers. At the same time it is more than simply a matter of symbols and ritual reflecting social arrangements and validating society as itself "sacred." The process, in my view, includes both of these aspects but is not limited to them. It is one of the essentials of human creativity, the capacity to generate categories and to endow with meaning various aspects of the endeavors of human life and not to endow other ones in the same way.

I write this book not so much so that I can explain an observed phenomenon to my audience of fellow anthropologists and other scholars but so that I myself can better understand this set of questions and shadowy answers. I write in order to put into words some of the exploratory guesses that have emerged from my encounter with ritual and symbolic expression in a cultural setting.

Here I guess, in part, that the processes of "secularization" in the West, especially the Protestant world and the world of industrialism and capitalism, have been accompanied by processes of "sacralization" of the town: The town has become home, mother, and protector, just as the church was once home, mother, and protector, but with an important difference. The town is made up of "citizens"; it creates in its civic self-construction the idea of the person as "detachable individual" who can leave or stay or alternate between them.

The town offers a passport to capitalism and colonialism, a temporary visa to remain away while retaining one's citizenship. Just as one says, "I belong to the church," one also says, "I belong to Selkirk," no matter how long one has remained at home or been away.

I explore these themes and guesses through the method of ethnography and the analytical perspective of ethnology. I look at symbolic expression, the relation of symbols to one another and to performance, and the relation of symbols and performance to social relations, social experience, and the social arrangements of everyday life.

I
THE COMMON RIDING

The common riding has been held faithfully in Selkirk for generations on the first Friday after the second Monday in June. In the drama that unfolds early on the common riding morning, the most spectacular aspect is the appearance of four or five hundred horses and riders following the royal burgh standard bearer down High Street, across the river, and around the boundaries of the old town's common lands. The horses are led outward by the town's silver band playing a medley of local songs in the same order and at the same places every year. After the band comes the stream of walkers in a pattern of segments, each behind the flag of a ceremonial organization—merchants, weavers, hammermen, fleshers, ex-soldiers, and colonials. These are then followed by the town citizenry overflowing into the streets in a flood of revelry and singing. Riders have arrived early from other towns, and Selkirk folk visiting from overseas have come to visit home, adding to the merriment and celebration. On the "nicht a'fore the morn" these folk all have followed the costumed bailie on foot around the streets bounding medieval Selkirk, with pauses at the site of each ancient "port" or gate to the town. Many have witnessed the solemn Flodden memorial and the laying of the wreath by ex-standard bearers.

The day begins at 5:00 A.M. with the first drum and then the singing of "Hail Smilin' Morn." By 9:00 the riders have ridden the marches and returned, coming up the hill at a gallop past the old toll, and ending their ride in the market square. There the burgh flag is handed back to the town's provost, and the young standard bearer ceremonially reports to the assembly that he is returning it "unsullied and untarnished." He reports that he has found all the boundary stones in the seven-mile perimeter to be in good and right order, undisturbed by the surrounding landowners, referred to as the "encroaching aristocracy."

Immediately before handing over the burgh flag, the flag casting of the guilds and the burgh is solemnly performed. In a powerful and beautiful dancelike motion of rhythm, strength, and skill, each standard bearer lifts above his head the large and heavy flag of his guild and waves the flag in a slow figure-eight motion, to the band's playing "Up wi' the Souters of

Selkirk," repeated over and over. The Union Jack, the British flag of the Ex-Soldiers' Association, is the last flag to be cast. At this point the music changes to a slow, poignant folk melody known as "The Liltin'," and the British flag is bowed to the ground in homage to the young men of the song entitled the "Flowers of the Forest" who died in the Battle of Flodden. The entire ceremony has formed, moved through its sequence of activities, and disbanded in a mere four hours' time. Yet the power and significance of these hours pervade the town's life throughout the year and over generations. It will be the subject of discussion in the street, in the Conservative Club and the Cricket Club, and will inform the reenactment of the same sequences and symbols each year on Common Riding Day for Selkirk.

1

Scenes of Heroes, War, and Death: Patriotism and Memorials

In all the Border towns, and particularly in the most ancient ones, a story woven into civic ritual is that of the Battle of Flodden, fought with the English in 1513, in which the Scots were the losers and their king was killed. The stories vary from town to town, but each has a local hero and many include the capture of an English flag. The Selkirk story involves Fletcher as its hero, and the scenes commemorative of war and the war dead revolve around his heroic presence. He is signified in a statue, in the person of the royal burgh standard bearer, in the soldiers who died in the First World War, and in the standard bearers of each ancient guild and two modern men's associations as they cast their flags. Each scene calls on imagery introduced in scenes before, and so I begin with a description of what actually happens as the performance begins.

The Fletcher Memorial

On a Thursday evening, the "nicht a'fore the morn" of the first Friday after the second Monday in June, the ex–standard bearers of Selkirk assemble quietly in a side street at an appointed hour to carry out their annual walk to the statue of Fletcher in High Street. The men are dressed in their best suits, each wearing the necktie of the Ex–Standard Bearers' Association. None wears an overcoat, even though the mist is almost always falling, and the chill of the evening is often bitter. The scene before the eyes of the visitor is one of eerie commemoration, equally recalling funereal pallbearers, soldiers in a close-order drill, and monks walking solemnly to their prayers. At the head of the procession is the current royal burgh standard bearer, who carries in his hand a memorial wreath to lay at Fletcher's feet in remembrance of the Battle of Flodden and the brave young men of Selkirk who died there. Behind him in double file walk the other ex–standard bearers in order of their year of honor. Behind the wreath bearer is the former provost of the town, the only ex–standard bearer to have had such an honor and the only one to come from a mill-owning family. Next to him walks a retired pattern weaver from the mill whose flag-carrying year was 1939. Behind them comes the re-tired town librarian who carried the flag in 1948 when many of the town's young men had gone away. The line goes on, including the local draper, a butcher, a mechanic, a shop owner, and numerous workers in woolen textile crafts and in building trades. The wreath is laid, and in silence the men disband.

If one asks a local worthy who watches from the sidelines with teary eyes what is going on here, just what the Fletcher ceremony is all about, he will answer with a story: "We do this because in 1513 all the young men of Selkirk went out to fight the Battle of Flodden. Only one man returned, carrying a captured English flag. He cast it in the market square and then fell down dead." If one presses for more details, the answers become diffuse; history merges with lore; and the facts are lost in the misty past. Fletcher reportedly was asked by the townsfolk for news of those who had fallen, but being "too grief-stricken to reply, . . . he swept the flag round in the manner of a scythe, indicating that the rest were slain," goes the story as told by one local historian. Another chronicler validates the facts of the tale and adds that it is this encircling motion that inspired the manner of the cast-ing of the colors in the market square as the climax of the common riding ceremonies.

The Fletcher statue, also known as the Flodden memorial, is a bronze statue of a soldier in armor carrying a flag. It stands in a promi-nent spot in front of the town's Victoria Hall in High Street. It was commissioned in 1913 to commemorate the four-hundredth anniver-sary of the battle, paid for by public subscription, and cast in bronze by a sculptor, Clapperton, whose home was in the Borders. The years of the statue's completion coincide with the years of Scotland's engagement in the First World War and the donation of Selkirk again of "all its young men," many of whom, like those of Flodden, never returned from battle.

As the ex–standard bearer lays the group's wreath at Fletcher's feet, all those around observe a "moment of silence in honor of the dead who died at Flodden," creating a sense of identification not only with the Flodden dead and the dead of the more recent wars but also with Fletcher, endowing him with the power to represent the town's heroic dead from all wars. In this ceremony and on the following day, Fletcher takes on an increasingly important role. He is the gallant in the return saga, calling up visions of the romantic days of knighthood and the glorious defense of honor. He stands for all heroes who died with honor, for all of Selkirk's fallen young men, as an example of objective generality.[1]

In the same sense, the royal burgh standard bearer becomes objectively general as he rides the marches on Common Riding Day carrying the burgh flag as each of these "veterans" has done. He represents Fletcher, who represents all those who died in battle and all those who returned. In order to be eligible to carry the town flag, a young man must be single; he must have served as an attendant in previous common ridings; and he must have been "born on the burgh soil." In addition, he must exhibit in his life and reputation all the characteristic virtues of the hero. Those young men chosen for the honor have traditionally been in their late twenties. After leaving Selkirk school, they have taken their places beside fathers and brothers who are trades and crafts specialists, and after the day of honor they have remained in the town to become its worthies.

In this ceremonial march, the double-file column of ex–standard bearers represents past rides and past encounters with dangers, and they are made up of those who have served the town well and have returned to take their places as pillars of the community. As tradesmen, shopkeepers, mill workers, and craftsmen in everyday roles, they stand for the populace over the years who have held the town's honor and ongoing life in their hands and have returned it in right and good order on this day. In their ceremonial position they represent the heroism of going into the margins of the world "outside" in carrying the flag around the town lands, and at the same time, they represent a safe return.

The flag that each of these men has carried over the years is the flag of the Royal and Ancient Burgh of Selkirk. It carries the burgh seal, depicting a young woman and her child. If asked to explain the emblem, the town residents will tell you a story of the return from

Flodden, in which Fletcher encountered a mother with her child on the roadside. Here is a version of the story that appears in one local history:

> Then there is the "legend of Ladywood Edge" which tells of Fletcher on his return as he topped a wooded ridge to the south of the town and heard the cry of a child. When he went to find the cause he was horror-struck to find an infant still suckling at its dead mother's breast. She was the wife of one who had been slain in the battle and she had died while keeping a futile vigil for his return. She and her child are immortalized in the Burgh Seal. (Harper 1985:7)

The young woman on the burgh flag is thought to symbolize the wives and mothers of soldiers over the centuries. By taking a small conceptual step, one sees her as representative of the town itself as the mother of the men, sending them out to war and awaiting their return. The death and life of the town are intricately connected with its entanglement in war and outmigration; the child may signify its hope of regeneration.[2]

The feelings of the standard bearer about the flag were reported by one ex–standard bearer to be similar to those a member of the regiment might feel about the battle flag: "You would like to protect it . . . in battle the troops are all following the flag . . . if troops got separated, they would look for the flag." This same speaker expressed deep reverence for the flag and its sacrosanct nature. He sees it as something resembling a holy object. In criticizing the younger people's lack of respect, he related a story of watching the flag-casting practice one evening and seeing that the burgh flag was not being treated with what he considered proper respect. "I got right put out about this," he said, "it's like somebody playing about with your wife!" This equation of the flag with the woman one loves is congruent with the notion of keeping the flag "unsullied and untarnished" and with the image of the town as a woman, a wife, a mother, who must be kept unstained and whose honor must be protected at all costs.

The use of the woman and child on the burgh flag echoes the central image of mother and child in Roman Catholic iconography and also the use of female iconography in republican imagery in the France of the Revolution—congruences that have not gone unnoted in the literature of symbolic analysis.

In his work on the French Revolution, Maurice Agulhon traces the use of the female image known as Marianne and later the "goddess of Reason" and the "goddess of Liberty," at various times used to represent the Revolution and the republic in France between 1789 and 1880. At first Agulhon finds the Marianne image as a peasant woman wearing a Phygian cap, the sign of a freed slave in Greek iconography. Later the republic was represented by a woman in classic garb draped with robes or a shawl and wearing a headpiece of grain (wheat, etc.) or a headpiece of a star, as in the American Statue of Liberty. She often carried the tract of *The Rights of Man* and sometimes a torch representing freedom (Agulhon 1981, 1985). The festivals described by Mona Ozouf also used the Marianne imagery, especially in the rural areas where groups carried plaster-of-paris dolls in form of Marianne, also goddesses of liberty in processionals for the festivals that replaced saints' days after the Revolution (Ozouf 1988). In Selkirk, a town that has lost great streams of its young people over the years to outward movement for war and emigration, it is not surprising that the woman on the flag is said to have been "waiting by the side of the road for soldiers to return."

One of the messages of the Fletcher story and its commemoration in the laying of the wreath by the ex–standard bearers is the message of heroism and honor in the face of death, a kind of romanticism woven in and through all the aspects of common riding imagery. The Fletcher story follows a pattern of the oldest romances (the *chansons de geste*) in which the death scenes, as described by Ariès in his study of Western attitudes toward death (Ariès 1974:3), include the hero's staging of his own death. In the *Chanson de Roland*, for example, Ariès finds a classic example of the traditional death ceremony of the hero. Roland remembers the lands he had conquered, "sweet France," the men of his lineage, Charlemagne, his lord who had nurtured him, and his master and companions (Ariès 1974:9). It is a romance of memory that focuses on honor in battle, nation, lineage under a feudal lord, and on male companionship.

In staging his death scene, Fletcher remembers the town and "all the brave men of Selkirk who died at Flodden." He returns with the captured flag to cast it in the marketplace as a signifier of honor in defeat. The Flodden story is also set in a romantic past for Scotland and marks the end of one phase of that romantic past, a romantic ending to the sovereignty of James IV and the beginning of a long period of wars with England over dominance and territorial integrity for Scotland.

The Fletcher statue is an example of objective generality, in that it represents to the people of Selkirk the men who have died in wars in defense of the nation and the town (the "nation" almost always carrying the referent of "Scotland" rather than "Britain," although recent wars were connected closely with the expansion or defense of the "British Empire"). This representation of Scotland by Fletcher is repeated in the emblematic figure of the standard bearer carrying the town flag around the boundaries. Milton Singer goes back to the writing of Pierce in his explanation of this concept in the following passage on the representation of the war dead from the American Civil War:

> A statue of a soldier on some village monument, in his overcoat and with his musket, is for each of a hundred families the image of its uncle, its sacrifice to the Union. That statue then, though it is itself single, represents any one man of whom a certain predicate may be true. It is *objectively general*. (Pierce 1955:263, quoted in Singer 1984:117; italics in original)

In Selkirk the Fletcher statue takes on this generality, while two other prominent statues on High Street, those of Sir Walter Scott and Mungo Park, remain merely commemorative. The standard bearer stands in this same relationship to the other mounted figures—for other riders in other times and places and essentially for the individual hero within the wholeness of the town, the one leader within and dependent on the total "battalion" of horsemen who follow.

The Act of Remembrance

On the next day after this ceremony, on Friday, the Common Riding morning, at the first light of dawn, there unfolds a second scene of war and remembrance. Near the market square at the center of the town stands the war memorial, a thin obelisk against the pale gray sky, where the ex-soldiers and members of the British legion assemble to pay their respects to their comrades in arms, the dead who died in the two world wars. The small crowd of early risers is sure to include the mothers and fathers of soldiers currently in the army, as well as the living kin of those honored in the long list of soldiers who perished in the 1914–18 conflict. Buried in their field of battle or in the far-flung territories of empire, generations of British war casualties have had only their names on monuments in village market squares to indicate their individuality in the collective slaughters of foot soldiers throughout the centuries. The sadness is present and poignant at the early morning service as the soldier-citizens are recognized for their supreme sacrifice for God and country and for town. The sound of taps cuts through the quiet of daybreak, and the service ends.

The British army has traditionally practiced a military convention of recruiting whole regiments from one geographic locality, a
practice in effect when the recruits went off to World War I. And so
it was that on one day in July 1915 the regiment known as the King's
Own Scottish Borderers (KOSB) was decimated at the Battle of Gallipoli. "The total casualties in the Fourth Battalion of the KOSB," according to one source, "amounted to 553 and few households in the
town escaped loss of one kind or another. It was Selkirk's 'second
Flodden'" (Roberts 1985:150). Selkirk, a town of 5,000, lost 292 men
in the First World War, each now remembered with his name on the
monument.

In telling of the impact of wars and war losses on the town of
Selkirk, local historian Stewart Roberts wrote the following account
comparing the loss and remembrance of three recent wars:

> While the Boer War is remembered in Selkirk only by the plaque on
> the Pant Well inscribed with the names of those who took part and
> by the name "Spion Kop," the First World War left a legacy which
> affected the town for more than a generation. . . .
>
> The First World War . . . had a most profound impact because of
> the terrifying scale of the casualties. The concentration of Selkirk men
> serving in the K.O.S.B.'s meant that the engagements in which these
> battalions were involved brought a series of numbing casualty lists to
> the town.
>
> By far the worst of these followed a disaster on 12–13 July, 1915,
> in Gallipoli. The total casualties in the Fourth Battalion of the K.O.S.B.
> amounted to 553 and few households in the town escaped loss of one
> kind or another. It was Selkirk's "second Flodden." For a number of
> years after the war a Sunday in July nearest the twelfth was observed
> as "Remembrance Day" and was an occasion of local mourning for
> those who fell on that day in 1915. The losses throughout this war
> rendered all too personal and poignant the closing tribute after the
> casting of the colours in the Market Place for many, many years.
>
> The Roll of Honour of the 292 who died during the war can be seen
> on the War Memorial erected in their memory. . . .
>
> In 1939 for the third time in the twentieth century Britain was
> involved in a war. In the Second World War many Souters gave their
> lives for King and Country on active service, and in the Merchant Navy,
> but fortunately casualties were on a much reduced scale when com-
> pared with the years 1914–1918. The total losses amounted to 44 of
> whom only ten were serving with the K.O.S.B. (Roberts 1985:150–51)

Roberts does not emphasize the shift in British policy from assigning men from one region to the same battalion, but this practice

did change the effect of devastating losses from one encounter in battle. Today the KOSB is an important military symbol for the Borderers, even though its service people come from all regions. At intervals throughout the year, one can read in the *Southern Reporter* of visits and KOSB ceremonial performances or marches, but the unit does not have a part in the displays connected to town festivals and common ridings. The images of the military are seen in the military formations of the ex–standard bearers and the laying of their wreath, the marching of the ex-servicemen to the war memorial and the laying of their wreath, in the military march-past style of the guilds behind their flags in the foot processional, and in the images of cavalry invoked by the horses as they ride out of the town and around the boundaries. Military motifs are overlaid with those of the church and the town in the mysterious blend of symbolism that has become associated with the creation of the "nation." It is displayed in this case as the merging of nation with the town as essentially a *civic* nationalism, and then the separation again of these entities into competing forces for the attention and the loyalty of subjects and citizens.

In light of the devastating effect of the war casualties throughout Scotland, it is not surprising that so much of the town ceremony in the Border towns is centered on representations of death in battle. Smout notes that the war was at one level perceived as mismanaged and disastrous, an intrusion by the powerful into the lives of the townsfolk.

> As a whole the First World War served as such an object lesson in the folly, remoteness, and even corruption of the rulers as to raise the class consciousness of the workers by several degrees—not certainly to the white heat of revolution but, undoubtedly, to a warm sense of disenchantment with those in power. This was fuelled, for one thing by the inept management of the war by the generals and the politicians. (Smout 1986: 267)

In discussing the number of Scots who died in war, Smout observes:

> One well-argued estimate put the figure at 110,000, equivalent to about 10 percent of the Scottish male population aged between sixteen and fifty, and probably to about 15 percent of total British war dead—the sacrifice was higher in proportionate terms than for any other country in the Empire. Thirteen out of fourteen were privates and non-commissioned officers from the working classes. . . . The anguish of war was countered in church by appeals to patriotic sentiment and other ecclesiastical bromides. The clerical Principal of Aberdeen University called it "a sacrament, and a sacrament in the full sense of that name as we Scots have been brought up to understand it." (Smout 1986: 267)

The sacramental nature of death as part of a little understood and distantly controlled war in the "outside world" was not an easy concept for the mothers and wives of Scottish soldiers to accept. And the mismanagement to which Smout refers was seen as further evidence of the hostile forces of the politicos, the nobles, the aristocrats, and the faraway London government in opposition to the interests of the simple working people in the Scottish towns. At the same time, it is not possible to consign one's sons and husbands to death in a war that is nonsensical. And so the losses of all wars in all times are invoked in the merger of recent collective slaughter with honorable and romantic valor in the misty past in the Battle of Flodden. In the glorious past, Scotland was clearly fighting for its own sovereignty against England's aggression. In the two world wars the sacrament of shed blood symbolizes a more painful reality of encounter with the world beyond the town.

The symbolic world of Reformed Protestantism in Scotland and among Scots-Presbyterians worldwide is one without elaborate emphasis on the dead or the death ritual. Instead, its universe is populated primarily by living persons whose afterlife is not in question, because they have already been "saved" by the previous Grace of God. Death ritual is intentionally austere, especially in the Reformed tradition that prefigures the modern Church of Scotland and its counterpart in the southeastern United States, the Presbyterian denomination. In the ritual marking of a person's death, the service focuses on the life of the individual and on the "Sovereignty of God." Ministers who follow closely this prescription discourage displays of ceremony or floral tribute and encourage a simple memorial service in the sanctuary of the church where the person has been a member.

This view of individual death and life in Protestant belief and practice is congruent with the gradual cognitive shifts accompanying the development of modern capitalism as seen by Weber and others; it reflects the shift from viewing the person as a member of a structured and bounded group to viewing the person as an individual pilgrim on a journey outward into a personalized and individualized existence within a modern, capitalistic world.[3] If the dead appear at all in this symbolic universe, it is as individuals whose memory is revered and whose lives are commemorated by individual gravestones, plaques, citations, or—in the case of those who have become particularly successful in the quest to seek their fortunes—individual memorials as statues, buildings, or churches carrying the name of an illustrious founder or donor.

The Protestant dead appear collectively in only two different semantic locations. One of these is in the kin group of ancestors in the American South. Ancestors are honored collectively by their descendants in the southern United States in the large kin-religious gatherings I have described as "rituals of reunion in American Protestant culture" (see Neville 1987a). These honored dead are the original Scottish and Scots-Irish emigrants and their descendants. It was these people who left Scotland or Ulster in the eighteenth and nineteenth centuries to settle in North Carolina, and it was their descendants who later moved to Tennessee and Texas. They were acting out the Protestant and capitalist imperative to leave home and "seek their fortune."

A second semantic location for Protestant dead as a collective is that of the dead who died in war. In the cultural complex common to Scotland and parts of North America, the war dead are honored in the various Memorial Day and Veterans Day ceremonies held in towns on both sides of the Atlantic. In war, as in emigration, young men went out from their homes into an unknown encounter with an enemy. In both cases, many never returned. Civic celebrations honoring the war dead have been documented by Warner (1961) and Davies (1955) in studies of Memorial Day in American towns, and evidence from the commemorations of the war dead in Europe suggests that memorial days of various kinds are part of the cultural universe of civic nationalism in general.

I do not claim that these are specifically Protestant or "capitalist." But I do point out some of the ways in which civic ceremonies honoring the dead and celebrating the sacredness of the town provide dramatic performances of otherwise invisible cultural themes that are especially powerful motifs of Protestantism and "modern life." These include the themes of individualism and personal fulfillment, in stark conflict with the coexisting themes of local belonging and local cultural identification against the "outside world." If the person is an individual free to leave home and wander the world of empire, the town as a locale must create an alternative bond pulling the immigrant "home" and at the same time constructing a meaning for those who remain behind. Death and life images are used in my example as expressions of individual death in war and emigration and also of the threatened death of the town through depopulation and invasion by the "other."

The common riding provides one such cultural expression of civic identity and symbolization in one long-term Protestant region, the Scottish Borders, which has been Reformed Protestant for over four hundred years. My interest in the civic ceremony described here goes far beyond its uses of death imagery and the honor of the dead. These additional interests include the role of symbols in the processes of social change and the transformation of Catholic, traditional symbolic worlds to Protestant, modern ones in Scotland and the United States. Here I have focused narrowly on representations of death as one element in this larger set of transformations in sacred and civic realms.

Death here is seen not only as the claimer of soldiers in war but also as the ever-present aggressor against the town itself; the breaker of the boundaries, the threat to social order and accustomed hierarchies; the enemy of tradition. It is the enemy against which all the town's young men ride out in military cavalcade each year, guarding against not only their own deaths but also the collective death of their town and its traditional ways.

2

Scenes of Processions, Marking of Boundaries, and Casting of Flags

The contact with the world beyond the town has produced further experiences of loss and death, especially loss through emigration and the threatened death of the town's autonomy through its sale of common lands and its loss of local political control. These themes are represented in the ongoing drama through the riding of the boundaries and the procession of the guilds. The horses and riders assemble in a street called Back Row and wait for the appointed hour as townsfolk begin to gather at 6:15 A.M. in High Street to sing the first of the common riding songs, to the music of the silver band. The singing throng makes its way to Victoria Hall, where they watch and cheer the handing over of the burgh flag by the provost to the royal burgh standard bearer for his ceremonial ride. By 7:00 A.M. the crowd is streaming into the streets in a merry surge of guilds behind their flags, with the riders following behind the standard bearer and his attendants, all adorned in stately garb with hunting jackets and fine attire festooned with rosettes in town colors, and the walking public singing loudly to the tunes they have known from childhood to be sung in a set order on Common Riding morning.

The foot procession winds its way through the streets, leads out the riders in the mounted processional, and then reassembles later to lead the riders back in. The processional is led by clusters of men walking as guilds behind the flag of each organization in a set traditional order, followed by the general townsfolk on foot. The loud singing and revelry accompanied by band music creates an atmosphere of enjoyment resembling the feast and the fair. In a starting-and-stopping process reminiscent of the Catholic processionals in which a chant or a prayer is sung at each "station," the civic parade marches gaily through its program into the midmorning, breaks while the riders go out around the commons, and then comes together again to end its trek at the market square at the ceremonial close.

The Guilds and the Colonial Society

The guilds marching in the processional are ceremonial men's associations whose stated function and meaning are connected with the common riding. These functions and meanings include not only the choosing of a guild standard bearer to carry and cast the guild flag and the marching together in the closed grouping behind that flag in the foot procession, but also the holding of a series of meetings, dinners, and receptions for months preceding and following the day of the celebration itself. Four guilds represent the ancient crafts, trades, and fixed position in medieval burgh life: the Hammermen, Merchants, Weavers, and Fleshers. A fifth represents the veterans of British armies and wars, the ex-servicemen; the sixth group is the Colonial Society, known also informally as the "exiles," which springs into action annually, orchestrated by local residents who were at one time "colonials," to welcome home those who have returned from overseas for Common Riding Day.

The imagery of death in war is joined here by the imagery of death through emigration and, even more deeply set, the meanings of the town's own death and life. These themes appear in the foot processional in the presence of the guild consisting of the temporarily returned "exiles" who live overseas after having forsaken the town to emigrate to the world beyond. Over the years emigration has drained the population of its source of growth and change; it has been just as devastating in taking away "all the brightest and the best" as was the devastation of Flodden and the two world wars. In receiving the returned emigrants—the "leavers"—into the town's central ceremonial time and assigning them a position with the ancient guilds, the "stayers" find a way of reconciling or attempting to reconcile sym-

bolically and ritually the ambivalent position of the town vis à vis
the emigration experience. Just as mothers and sisters wept for the
losses in war, mothers and sisters wept for their family members who
left for the colonial world, many never to return. As the tears are shed
for Flodden and the dead of the world wars, the tears are also shed for
the absent children and relatives who will never be back for the common riding. This same theme of social death and loss is extended into
the concern over the social death of the town itself, represented symbolically in the discourse of protecting the town from encroachments
and in the elaborate processual metaphor of riding around the boundaries of the common lands.

The ancient guilds stand for an older, more traditional Selkirk,
which in feudal times was the holder of rights granted only by the
king, which as a royal burgh had privileges not held by other villages
or trading centers. The merchants were the group who held the privilege of being burgesses in this older order; the hammermen held the
closely guarded trade positions of mason, cooper, wright, joiner, gla-
zier, and smith. The weavers began as important skilled specialists
and continued as significant craftspeople in the heyday of the woolen
textile mills. The fleshers were handlers and purveyors of meat. Other
trades and crafts abounded, including the locally significant one of
"souter" or shoemaker, which gave Selkirk its residents' nickname.

Each of the craft and trade brotherhoods became incorporated in
the 1500s or 1600s, becoming, like the town, an instance in which
an individual could be separate as a "member" and "brother" yet part
of an incorporated group that was secular instead of sacred. Even
though the guilds were technically secular, they give evidence of
another fusion of symbols from religious and civic realms. Each brotherhood evolved its own rituals, meeting in a "lodge" or special club
room, and even into the early nineteenth century held assigned group
seating areas in the parish kirk, emblazoned with guild imagery long
after the Reformation. The resemblance of trade guilds in medieval
and early modern times to Roman Catholic religious orders presents
an intriguing subject for further exploration. The central ceremonial
role of the guilds in the common riding is long standing, and the guilds
and their flags continue as powerful symbolic forces in and through
the local community.

The addition of the two modern men's ceremonial societies to
the civic ritual observance further continues the process of merging
religious and civic ideology and practice as part of the ceremonial
accommodation of corporate tradition to individual choice. The town
remained essentially a medieval burgh in all aspects of its life and

social organization, with a set of clear-cut, fixed, transgenerational position, until the coming of the woolen mills in the 1830s (see Gulvin 1973: 88–89). Industrial growth changed the town forever, adding thousands of incomers from the valleys and villages who became mill workers, disturbing the delicate balance of traditional trades and crafts. The town was forced to change again at the century's turn, when world wool prices dropped and the United States imposed stringent tariffs on Scottish textiles. It was at this turn that the mills began to close, jobs disappeared, and the outward drain of emigration to the larger British Empire took its toll.

In documenting the effect on town life of these forces from the "outside world," one local historian notes that "in the 40 years from 1841 until 1881 the population increased from 1,675 to 5,977. Incomers to the town made up the bulk of the increase, drawn by the mills and the prosperity of the textile trade" (Brown 1985: 147). These changes were, of course, not entirely negative for the townsfolk. Jobs provided new sources of prosperity; housing was expanded and improved by developers seeking to gain profit from the influx; and town services were significantly modernized. Local people embraced the prosperity while coping with the accompanying disturbance of prestige and power relations. The woolen mills ruled the Borders during these golden years for the textile trade, and most of the existing Selkirk was constructed during the late nineteenth century.

The boom years were ended by the turn of the century in 1900. One local writer, a chronicler of the woolen industry, describes the collapse:

> There was a serious depression in the 1890s when trade with America almost came to a standstill following the imposition of a series of very heavy duties on imports. Exports of cloth from Galashiels to America declined from 500,000 in 1889 to 50,000 by 1900. The recession gave rise to an acceleration in emigration to the Dominions and to the U.S.A. (Roberts 1985a:118)

The two types of men's organizations at the common riding allow for an expression of the old town's coping with encroaching modernization. The ancient guilds no longer functioning as economic entities represent the older order; the newer ones existing in response to individual choices and involvement in world economic and political struggles represent a world of change.

The imagery of Marianne from the French Revolution is a figure that may be profitably mentioned again in connection with the guilds and their persistent representation of themselves in the ceremonial garb of the mysteries and secret symbols associated with Masonic traditions and rituals. The early peasant Marianne, according to Maurice Agulhon, became identified with radical movements in later nineteenth-century France (1850–80), chiefly in Paris and southern France. She wore a red cap and the insignia of communes and labor movements and also, especially in the South, those of secret societies known as "Mariannes." The Marianne imagery was also associated with the imagery of the Masonic movements. All these forces and groups were staunchly anticlerical and anti-Catholic (Agulhon 1981). In Scotland the Masonic movement has historically been a strong local organization.

The presence of Masonic imagery and ritual themes in the common riding is seen in the guild brotherhoods as "lodges" and their separate assemblages for drinking and dining before and after the common riding together in affirmation of their trades and crafts. It is also seen in the symbolism itself of the segmented foot processional, the carrying of flags as banners, and the symbolism of death and renewal of life. It is in keeping with the historic location of protest in secret societies and brotherhoods. In the absence of unions in Selkirk, the only focal point for organized opposition—even if it is chiefly symbolic opposition—is found in the guilds and men's societies. It is interesting that there is no group marching in the common riding behind a flag or banner of the Masons. This is a powerful statement of silence. The men's brotherhoods represent aspects of the same type of brotherhood, enshrouded in the secrecy of the Masonic veil. The common riding resembles one large Masonic-type ritual, enacting secret ongoing resistance to the aristocracy, the clergy, and the generalized establishment represented in the "outside world."

In the fusion of images from the populist festival—liberty, equality, and fraternity—the local town, not the nation or the church, is here the object of loyalty. This is civic pride at the town, not the national, level, in which the nation and its distant powers are represented by the encroaching dukes and earls, just as in France the kings and princes were associated with the ancien régime. In this representation, Selkirk is personified as a woman weeping for her lost sons and also as a woman whose virtue requires protection by the vigilant defense of the standard bearer and his followers in the guilds.

In one of those curious inversions in which culture is enacted and expressed in festivals and in serious rituals of all kinds, the Masonic ritual, which is so clearly anti-Catholic, calls on and repeats elements of Catholic ritual and liturgical form in its own ritual construction, that is, in robes, banners, processionals, images of death and life and dark and light, the use of torchlight parades, and elaborate ceremonialism in general. In the same fashion, the common riding's ritual and liturgical form, clearly antiaristocracy, calls on images drawn from its antithesis: the mounted cavalcade of riders dressed in the attire of the hunt, the imagery of the military parade and the "tattoo," and the references to local principals as "royalty" in some towns and, in others, in terms otherwise reserved for gentry and nobility. And in increasing circles of complexity, the common riding itself uses the pageantry and liturgy of Catholicism in making statements about nonhierarchical social orders and antiestablishment meanings, which is a Protestant use of Catholic ritual to make statements about the contradictions of life lived between tradition and modernization.

This study is not intended to delve into the mysteries of Masonic ritual or to claim that the common riding is an overt transformation of Masonic forms. Such a thesis would require yet another body of research and another book on the subject itself. It is significant, however, that a number of similarities do exist in the two forms of ceremony, and so I point out these as one aspect of the way that symbolic inventories within a cultural setting can be combined and recombined over time for various meanings and various purposes. Mona Ozouf discovered this congruence between Masonic symbolism and the symbolism of the French revolutionary festivals. Her discussion of these similarities and concurrent symbolic expressions has convinced me that the same kinds of borrowings and repeated cultural themes pertain to the symbolism and ritual process of the common riding. She wrote the following about the festivals in postrevolutionary France: "We are discovering, beyond even the borrowings from Masonic symbolism, the profound kinship between the Masonic ritual and the Revolutionary festival: in both Masonry and in the Revolution, every assembly is ipso facto a festival" (Ozouf 1988:277). And about the music of the two festival-performances, she went on to say:

> The composers used by Revolutionary authorities had almost all been initiated into lodges before 1789 as had the singers and the instrumentalists. . . . The Revolutionary music bore the mark of the as yet little known Masonic music, of which one may distinguish four kinds: the lodge concert, the Masonic song, the musical ritual, and the column of harmony. (Ozouf 1988:346)

According to Ozouf, who cites the work of Roger Cotte on Masonic music and that of Jacques Brengues (1974) on Masonic symbolism in the revolutionary festivals, one of the features of this musical tradition is the dialogue between a soloist and an all-male choir, the primary vocal group. A column of harmony is a group of wind instruments that, before the Revolution, consisted of two clarinets, two horns, and two bassoons, with the "possible multiplication of parts." "The requirements of the Masonic ritual established the practice of treating the wind instruments as the major if not exclusive, members of the orchestra." And Ozouf claims that "the Masonic influence on the very texture of the music used by the revolutionaries can be seen in the widespread use of such purely musical devices as triple time" (Ozouf 1988:346).

One cannot ignore the centrality of all-male choruses in common riding singing, especially in the ceremonial dinners of the guilds and ex–standard bearers before and after the festival weekend itself. These rowdy assemblies are accompanied by strong voiced singing of the all-male members assembled, sometimes using the dialogic format just described.

On Common Riding Day the silver band—composed of the wind instruments described earlier—takes on an important role, leading the parade of guilds and followers down the streets and out to the edge of the town with the set pattern of common riding songs that have special meaning for the town. A specialist in ethnomusicology, or a folklorist with a musical bent, would have material for several dissertations on this common riding music and its performance context. Indeed, several folklorists from Edinburgh have become interested in common riding songs and stories over the years, especially for the Langholm Common Riding. Recordings have been made by these people and also by professional recording teams in each town who then put the songs onto 33-rpm records or cassette tapes for sale in the local music stores. Every person in the town of Selkirk knows "by heart" all the words of each common riding song. They are taught and sung in the local schools and rehearsed informally at every local drinking club as the celebration grows near. There are special songs for the Colonial Society which deal particularly with Selkirk as home and with romantic images of the Borderland, its people, its "soft golden tongue," and return to "my ane folk."

The musical tradition associated with the common riding is old and deep in Border lore, with some songs coming from ballads and others from the pen of late nineteenth-century composers. In Selkirk, many well-loved tunes were composed by a local bandmaster, Christopher Reekie. In Hawick some of the songs come from an opera written by a local man who emigrated to Canada. The content of the songs and the date of their composition or the measure of the "authenticity" are only two elements of interest here. Far more significant in the study of symbols and symbolic process is the way in which the songs themselves are performed, in what sequence, by whom, when, and where, and in what sort of liturgical form connected to what other kinds of liturgies. To illustrate the apparent connections— what Ozouf calls "kinship"—of Masonic ritual to common riding ritual, I have focused briefly on the musical aspects of the common riding and some of its elements.

One final note on Masonic symbolism before leaving this excursion into symbolic convergences. This note relates to the ideal of the "Temple of Reason" in Masonry, referring to the tradition of enlightenment, truth, light, and rationality. Emblems of building and engineering predominate in the Mason's visible insignias, including the emblem of the builder appearing on Masonic lodges, gravestones, and badges of membership. The trades and crafts in Selkirk known as the "united crafts" or as "hammermen" represent this tradition of progress and careful, logical building of towns, preceded in history by the building of the abbeys, during which period some say the Masons got their start. The Hammermen is the guild that marches first in the procession at the common riding, an order dictated by the Edinburgh Council of Burghs in the eighteenth century.[1]

The collected trades of mason, carpenter, plasterer, joiner, glazer, and others all are included in the crafts and trades that are proud to have built the town of Selkirk over and over through the centuries as one phase fell down or was torn down to be replaced by a more prosperous or more "modern" version of townness. The trade guilds were especially active in the late nineteenth century after the arrival of the woolen textile mills. Most of the Selkirk that one sees today was built during this period, and much of the town remains the same as it was then. The hammermen hold a dinner and a concert before Common Riding Day, in which they observe the same ritual traditions as do the other guilds: the honoring of their standard bearer, the "bussin' of the flag" by a chosen lady, speeches of honor to the crafts and the town, a concert by soloists, and singing by the assembly of attenders. After the common riding, they, like the other guilds, hold a "foy," the occasion for revelry and song. On the hammermen's flag are a measuring rule, a saw, and other assorted tools, two of which prominently displayed are the emblems of the masons—the compass and the carpenter's square.

In all these rich comparisons of and searches for similarities and transformations, it is important to keep in mind that the Masonic

ritual and the common riding ritual are not of interest only because
one has borrowed from the other or that cultural traits and symbolic
materials persist over time and take on different expressions. Rather,
the two rituals are of interest here because they both very likely express in performance and bring into visibility some deeply rooted, frequently invisible cultural structures, processes, and meanings shared
in the traditions of Western European Christianity over time and
space. When speaking or writing of "Catholics" and "Protestants,"
one often forgets to note that these two cultural worlds are part of
one overall world of Christendom and that many of the traits and
specific forms we associate with Protestantism were not invented at
the Reformation, nor was civic ritual invented during the French
Revolution or in the royal burghs of twelfth-century Scotland. Culture is a perplexing concept, especially the culture and cultures of
highly textualized and highly liturgized Western Europe. The weight
of the commentary tends to drag us into forgetting that even these
"civilized" cultural forms share regularities of human cognitive life
and meaning-construction with all humans and their cultures
throughout our species' life.[2]

Following the hammermen in the procession are other brotherhoods. The guild of weavers was incorporated in the early seventeenth
century in Selkirk and represents those whose skill was cloth making, a cottage industry long before the advent of the Industrial Revolution. In writing about the textile industry in the Borders, Roberts
states:

> The Incorporation of Weavers, founded in 1608 had but 22 members
> in 1809. One of the main objects of the craft was to protect their own
> indigenous trade and the attitude of craft members was not conducive
> of an expansive response to the rapid increase in manufacture of woolen
> goods in neighbouring areas which had begun to develop about 1777.
> (Roberts 1985a:107)

The Corporation of Weavers, along with the other craft specialties in
these early years, operated primarily to protect their monopoly on
their trade and to exclude the persons from the "outside" who sought
to introduce newer techniques. Even then, a great deal of this activity was carried out by elaborate ritual ceremonies. As water-driven
and then power-driven looms began to catch on in the Borders, the
Selkirk weavers gradually adapted their guild to become the association of those who were skilled in the weaving craft, whether industrial or nonindustrial, while continuing their ceremonial reinforce-

ment of this exclusiveness. The highest status in the guild of weavers belongs to those whose particular task requires the most complex training and apprenticeship—the designers, pattern weavers, and other cloth specialists of today who continue to be important to the woolen textile–manufacturing process. Every position on the mill floor has a particular position and place. Both the deacon of the weavers and the chosen standard bearer of the guild must be men of high status and well thought of by their fellows.

Of the brotherhoods marching in the common riding procession, ne of those most closely guarding the older tradition of closed cororate burgh life is the Merchant Company. This company represents ie tradition of the burgesses of the old town past, in which only those ho were designated as burgesses might own property, collect tolls, id graze their cattle on the common lands. One such merchant is ι business on High Street in a shop that his father and his grandfather oth had held. He recalls that they had had the same space since 1862, nd before that, another space nearby. His father and his grandfather oth were burgesses; that is, he says that "they could graze their cattle on the town land—then at night brought the cows in through one loor—cows and people—cows to the back pens." He remembers the Selkirk of his boyhood:

> Back in those days it was really important to be the standard bearer. Everyone knew everyone else . . . 80 percent of the town was Selkirk (born on the burgh soil). . . . Now only about 20 percent is Selkirk. Then there were no fortnight holidays for the mills. Common Riding was *it.* . . . Back in those days the common riding was the centerpiece of the entire year.

The Merchant Company today represents the ceremonial interests of those who own shops and businesses. The history of Selkirk places the position of the merchant group as one at the top of the social and economic ladder as early as the twelfth and thirteenth centuries In his history of the town, Gilbert states that

> merchants became the wealthiest people in the burgh. In many burghs they formed their own guild or friendly society. . . . During the fourteenth century the merchants gained more power because they, through export customs, contributed to the wealth of the kingdom and were more able to contribute to the ransoms of David II and James I. By the fifteenth century there had developed a well defined distinction of merchants and craftsmen, and it was becoming exceedingly rare for craftsmen to become burgesses. The merchants alone could become bur-

gesses so they controlled the court, they selected the baillies and they monopolised trade. . . . The traditional picture, therefore, is one of hostility between merchants and craftsmen with merchants, because of their wealth, getting government backing to exclude craftsmen from all political and economic power. (Gilbert 1985:39)

The power of the merchants and the burgesses was broken by the Burgh Reform Act passed by Parliament in 1833, an act that coincided almost perfectly with the opening of the Galashiels road and the coming of the woolen textile mills to Selkirk. The Merchant Company retains its ceremonial significance in the face of these major changes in the town's social order.

The "closed" societies of hammermen, weavers, and merchants—closed to all but those men who have been initiated through craftsmanship in each particular guild—are complemented in the foot procession and casting of flags by the two "open" societies, the ex-soldiers and the colonials. Of these two, the Ex-Soldiers' Society is itself closed to all but those who have served in the British forces and, in Selkirk, is open only to men. The Colonial Society, in contrast, is closed only to those who have stayed at home. The members of the Colonial Society are those who have returned for the common riding march in the procession, along with those who left home to wander the globe in either war or emigration and have come home to live in Selkirk. The Colonial Society is of particular interest because of its role in structuring the return saga for the emigrants, in preparing a place for them within the town's social order.

Jack Harper, a returned émigré who has had a major hand in continuing the Colonial Society, dates its formation to 1910 in Guelph, Ontario, where he says that thirty people started the association known as the Selkirk Colonial Society. Every year they chose one member to come back for the common riding and cast the flag of the colonials. In the common riding of the 1990s, the colonial flag is cast by a person chosen in Selkirk by the society made up now of a number of returnees who accept the task of organizing the correspondence, the dinner, and the surrounding events. An advertisement is placed in the *Saturday Advertiser* (known locally as the "wee paper") for all those who wish to apply to be the colonial standard bearer in order to, according to Harper, "see who is coming home."

By the end of April the standard bearer has been chosen, and preparations are under way. Friends and relatives of that person pass along the word, and often a large group of Selkirk people return from the adopted home of the standard bearer. Harper notes that the all-time high in numbers was when sixty to sixty-five people "came home" when there was a colonial standard bearer from Canada, and about forty people came on a charter flight from Canada. In 1986 the greatest number were from New Zealand because there was a colonial standard bearer from New Zealand. Of his own experience as an "exile," Harper relates that he went out as a young man to work in the mines in Sierra Leone with two other Selkirk men and a "Hawick chap."

By far the greatest number of Selkirk emigrants move to Canada, New Zealand, or Australia. This phenomenon is attributable to various factors, including the moving of clusters of workers through the years to join mills and other woolen textile–related enterprises in places where Border companies had branched out, such as a very large contingent to Dunedin, New Zealand, with the Roberts Mill in the 1890s, and another cluster of Borderers to Lawrence, Massachusetts, at the turn of the century, when a local woolen mill opened a branch in the United States.

An additional factor is the process of chain migration. Through the exchange of letters and return visits, those who have been successful in the new land recruit their age-mates and family members to join them in the place where they have been successful. It is often pointed out in Selkirk that "only those who are successful ever come back for the common riding. There are a lot of them (the leavers) we never see again."

An example of the interconnectedness of common riding ceremonialism and the emigration experience can be seen in the headlines for the June 7, 1990, common riding page of preview and advertising in the *Southern Reporter*, headed "Selkirk Ready for Its Family Reunion." One family holding its own regathering in the 1990 event was the Russells, whose colonial standard bearer was "Murray Russell from Toronto . . . and he will be the last in the line of Russell brothers to have Cast the Colours at Selkirk." The *Southern Reporter* states:

> His brother Harry (52) was Royal Burgh Standard Bearer in 1965, so for him it will be the Silver Jubilee. And the other two Russell brothers have borne the Colours of the Crafts, so Murray will complete the quartet.
>
> What makes the family feat even more remarkable is that their father—who is now 86, will be there to oversee proceedings.
>
> . . . My brothers and I got together and we thought it would be great for my father to see the last of us Casting the Colours. . . . My brother Murray—who emigrated about 11 years ago—has come over for the Common Riding five or six times. (*Southern Reporter*, June 1, 1990, p. 13)

The colonial bussin' and reception in 1978 began with the public ceremony in Victoria Hall, welcoming fifty-nine visitors from overseas. Most of these were Australian, then Canadian, with only seven of the fifty-nine from the United States. In Victoria Hall all the visitors were seated on the stage in front of an audience of their Selkirk friends and relatives. There were speeches, welcomes, and the attaching of the 1978 ribbon to the colonial flag by the wife of the standard bearer for the society. There were both solos and group songs. The visitors were introduced and applauded. Then the group adjourned to the private part of the ceremony, a "reception" that was essentially a seated evening meal, a kind of "supper" in a private function room. Here the toasts began. There were memorial statements to the people who had died since the last common riding, to the war dead, and to Flodden.

The passage of time was a recurrent theme, as were also the stories featuring the town as a center of the exiles' symbolic world, especially the world of memory. In one story a man from Hawick who had gone away remembered High Street as being "a mile wide and three miles long." In another, a woman from Canada spoke of having returned to Selkirk for the first time since her childhood, when she was four or five years old. She thought Selkirk "was just a dream," and, she avowed, "It is every bit as lovely as I imagined." In another story, a woman from Illinois recalled having received common riding tapes every year from relatives. Another man, an elderly gentleman from Australia, told his story of having returned to the common riding fifty years after he had left and this year, six years later, being able to return yet again. All the songs sung at this gathering were nostalgic songs such as "My Ane Folk" and other songs recalling home.

Each of the Border towns has the tradition of returning exiles during the week of its town celebration. In Galashiels at Brawlads Day, there is a dinner known as Overseas Night; in Langholm the residents say that their relatives who are trying to plan a trip home always try to be there for the common riding. Only Selkirk claims to have a Colonial Society, at least a society with that name and one that is self-supporting, they say, with money that comes in from the tickets at the bussin' and from donations.

One of the anecdotes repeated at dinners is that "when two Englishmen meet overseas, they form a cricket team; when two Welshmen meet, they form a choir; and when two Scots meet, they form a Caledonian society." This could be extended to the Borderers who meet overseas and form a Borders association in their new home. One such group of former Selkirk folk met regularly for a common riding in Melbourne, Australia, under the leadership of a former Selkirk man who was the son of the famous bandmaster who composed many of the local songs. Chris Reekie was remembered in an obituary in the *Southern Reporter*:

> In setting out for a new life in Australia in 1922, Chris carried with him to his fresh pastures the rich attributes which had endeared him to the folk in Selkirk, and was soon to win the same recognition there.
>
> In his heart, however, he never forsook his native town and he became one of the pillars of the Colonial Society. His annual donation was handsome, and always the first to arrive, and at the Common Riding he held a Selkirk Night in Melbourne for all who were able to attend. . . . Never to become "well off," Chris nevertheless gave a helping hand to many a Borderer arriving as an immigrant—no one will ever know the number who owe a debt of gratitude to Chris Reekie or to what extent.
>
> In 1966 and at 73 years of age he was able to make the long-dreamed-of trip home to Selkirk for the Common Riding. . . . On the occasion of his 90th birthday, his friends organized a great party for him, and there were greetings by card and by audio cassette from many friends and organizations in Selkirk. (*Southern Reporter*, March 27, 1986, p. 2)

To demonstrate Chris Reekie's feelings for his natal home, the author of the obituary column, Jack Harper, quotes from a poem written by Reekie entitled "Exile." Harper notes that "in it he seems to connect the hereafter with Selkirk, suggestive of the ancient Scottish belief that at death the spirit returns by 'the low road' to the birth place."

I quote here Reekie's poem as reprinted in the *Southern Reporter* in his obituary:

EXILE
Yestreen I wandered down the years—
A rugged path called "Memory Lane,"
Where joys and sorrows, hopes and fears
In fancy, led me Home again.
The passing years, both sad and gay,
And memories that bless and burn
Surged through my soul. They seemed to say
"This is the day of your return."
I pondered, and beheld the smile
Of friends I knew in days of yore.
While others—loved and lost awhile
Had safely reached the farther shore.

My eyes beheld the heathclad hills:
The bonnie burn, and winding road:
The streets and lanes: The busy mills—
A breath of Home!
A glimpse of God!

(*Southern Reporter*, March 27, 1986, p. 2)

The Riding of the Boundaries of the Common Lands

At the heart of the celebration of its civic presence, Selkirk rides the boundaries of its old town's common lands in a processional of horses behind the royal burgh standard bearer. When the standard bearer is handed the flag by the provost in the early morning, he is sent on his way with the farewell "Safe oot, safe in." The perambulation of the seven-mile boundary is staged in such a way that several scenes of apparent danger provide drama to the unfolding day and offer the standard bearer and his followers opportunities to display their bravery in the face of threats. One of these is the crossing of the River Ettrick which, it is said, is subject to flooding; another is the "galloping in at the toll," a steep hill at the reentry into the town's streets. Further drama is provided by the horses' filing around the bounds at the top of an especially visible hill rim, so that onlookers from far away gain a sense of suspense and pageantry. The riders return to the market square, and at the end of the ceremony the burgh flag is returned to the provost with the report that the boundary stones are in place, "in good and right order," and that the flag is being returned "unsullied and untarnished." The town is again made safe for tradition.

The standard bearer appears at the head of the cavalcade, larger than life, the hero defending the burgh. As they have framed the events so far, the Fletcher figure, the images of Flodden, and the wars spill over and become superimposed on the young soldier hero encircling the boundaries to protect his home and way of life. The encirclement of the boundaries is the encirclement of the known and possessed world, in opposition to the world beyond, unknown and impossible to control.

The protection of the commons was a historical and legal necessity in the early centuries of the burgh's past. The original charter from King David in the twelfth century is said to have contained the gift of the common lands, with the specific directive that the boundary stones be checked and the limits perambulated annually. The surrounding landowners are said to have been guilty, over the years, of "encroaching" on the commons by moving the boundary markers to suit their purposes. Especially implicated is the duke of Buccleuch, whose estate surrounds the lands of Selkirk today and also many of the other Border towns. He and other nobles, aristocrats, gentry, and industrial land barons all have become lumped together as the "encroaching aristocracy" against whom the town must be protected. It is not accidental that the members of this group also are heads of government faraway in London, commanded regiments of Borderers in poorly conceived military campaigns, and often organized colonial enterprises. It is also they who historically consorted together to introduce the changes that have eaten away at the commons as a town-owned entity and have eroded the control by the town council of its own affairs. The boundaries of the ancient common lands have shrunk considerably over the centuries as the council sold off parcels to the large landowners and the developers of woolen mills. The boundaries since have become symbolic of the marking off of Selkirk as a traditional system of cultural meanings and behaviors from those forces "outside" that might seek to encroach on it.[3]

In addition to its symbolic encirclement of burgh life in opposition to the life associated with the large estates of gentry, aristocracy, nobility and royalty, the boundary riding is a statement against outside control by Parliament and absentee bureaucracy. It represents the idea of town government against the regionalization of local government by Parliament, which in 1973 began combining towns and counties into districts and regions. Through this "regionalization," the towns lost their local councils and provosts. Their governments were combined into various district offices scattered around the region. In the common riding the provost appears in full regalia for the one time each year, and the Common Riding Trust surfaces as a present-day ceremonial expression of the old town council. One ex-standard bearer, another of my "local experts," who had himself served numerous terms as an elected town councilman and provost, bemoaned the loss of local government by his pointing out that in the new system, elected officials to the district and regional council could be "total incomers," and in fact, at this time many are. He went on in an indignant manner: "These people, you see, have no connection whatsoever to Selkirk!"

This same venerable elder statesman described the process of modernization and boundary crossing that typifies the new Border towns as "Texanization." Among the government professionals and new mill management class, it is economical and trendy to live in one town and drive to work or concerts and festivals in another. And this practice speeds along the de-Selkirkization and de-localization;

it reflects the "new" Borders—"improved," "modernized," and "brought into the mainstream of the Scottish economy."

The traditional version of trans-Borderland boundary crossing was done by the aristocrats and gentry in the fox hunts and grouse-shooting parties, during country-house weekends and the seasons in London of the dukes of Roxburghe and Buccleuch and their households, and by earlier incomers (such as Sir Walter Scott) maintaining ties to Edinburgh or other places on the "outside." These are echoed in the boundary crossing of the new ruling class of managers and professional elites who move about with haste and efficiency and whose loyalties are national, regional, or corporate. In contrast, the ritual riding of the boundaries state for Selkirk the continued, idealized, safe in-group that continues to see itself as rooted solidly in the local community whose figurehead is born on the burgh soil.

Although the riders on Common Riding Day may include members of this stigmatized category of "others," only those who know that they are "ourselves" are eligible to hold places of honor, to serve in the planning and staging, to become marshals and attendants, to visit other town ceremonies representing Selkirk, and to know without a mistake each and every movement in the day's stage business and the lines of the day's prescribed songs and tales. On this day the local folk don the apparel preferred by the hunt and the gentry; they rent horses and sometimes clothes; they save for months or years to afford to field their sons as candidates for standard bearers; and they spend their savings on ceremonial food and drink and festivity. And through the staging and the display, they delineate themselves inside the boundaries of the burgh and bound the incomers out.

Part of the common lands whose boundaries are perambulated on the annual ceremony are the farms owned by the town, to the north of the town itself. The riders pause at the markers of "Linglie Hill," the "Three Brethren Cairn," and a spot designated as "Tibbie Tamson's Grave." The commons formerly extended far beyond these boundaries. In his booklet outlining the Selkirk traditions of "The Common, the Flag, and the Song" (which he calls the "Trinity"), Harper provides maps of the Selkirk marches for 1536 and 1681 in comparison with the ones ridden today. He observes the following about the common lands:

> The Selkirk Common as defined in the 1535 Charter extended to something like 11,200 acres comprising 5,400 acres to the north with 14 miles of march, and 5,800 acres to the south with almost 20 miles of march. Compared to a grand total of 34 miles in 1535, the length of march ridden today is approximately 6½ miles. (Harper 1985:5)

The importance of the town's common land cannot be under-estimated in its symbolic significance for the town's identity. In the royal burghs and the burghs of barony, the town commons became, early on, the point of ownership and status, setting them off from their neighboring villages and "farmtouns," in which no official charters and no official town ownership of town land existed. The tradition of how the common riding began in Selkirk and in other towns owning common lands is that it began with the requirement for the burgh law men (later shortened to "burleymen") to ride round the commons in order to protect the boundaries. In fact, there were numerous disputes over the years in which town officials encountered the henchmen of the lairds and fought over a boundary marker. One such incident is reported in town records for the slaying of a Selkirk official, John Muthag, by the Ker family or its representatives. In one of the official speeches for a dinner associated with the common riding, the speaker in 1990 called for a special stop on the riding to honor this man.

> John Muthag was Selkirk's first civic head to carry the title of Provost and with Baillie James Keith the pair were slain on their way to the courts in Edinburgh to settle a boundary dispute in 1541.
>
> Their murder reminds us of the reason we ride the Marches to this day. (*Southern Reporter*, June 14, 1990, p. 4)

In the same newspaper on the Common Riding Week of 1990, local historian Walter Elliot reminded the readers of the importance of the common riding tradition:

> In the medieval past, the Riding of the Common Lands was a necessary part of the burgess duties. Failure to turn out could result in a fine or being deprived of burgess rights of buying and selling within the burgh. Thus it was to the advantage of every burgess to turn out to make secure his share of the Common Lands. This was no small inheritance, for the burgh's Common Lands could be large, as in the case of Selkirk, where twenty-two thousand acres were held as late as the middle 1500s. This vast area drew the envious eyes of neighbouring lairds who would try to move markers to their own advantage. . . .
>
> It is noteworthy that the oldest continuous Common Riding, that of Selkirk, does not have a Right and Left Hand Man. The Standard-bearer is guided by Senior and Junior Burleymen (or Burgh-law men) and the mounted procession is known as The Burley. (*Southern Reporter*, June 14, 1990, p. 4)

Other speakers in other towns compare, as does Elliot, the "continuous" (some say "real") common ridings with those that have been invented or rediscovered in recent years. The four ridings that are said to be "real" (Selkirk, Lauder, Langholm, and Hawick) all are based on the ownership of common lands and are centered on themes of protecting the boundaries. The other Border festivals are said by these towns to be "synthetic." One important figure in the Langholm Common Riding expressed the difference in this way: "Galashiels has no possessions, no common land. Well, they can mix up their red and white roses, they can have their piece of sod and piece of rock [scenes in the staging of Brawladsday in Galashiels]. But they don't have any boundaries." The same speaker went on to elaborate on the attempts of the regional governments to do away with all this: "They [the regional councils] have no respect for boundaries. They think that boundaries are relics of something stupid. . . . Common riding is pride in communal possession!"

It is noteworthy that the regional government's authority in 1975 may have indeed understood the power of communal possession and, for this very reason, sought early in the regionalization process to end the Border ridings. As it turned out, the attempt was unsuccessful, and after a short period of keeping the town robes and chains of office impounded in town museums or libraries, the regional and district authorities were forced to admit defeat and to allow the provost's robes and chains to be worn on ceremonial days only and to designate one person in the town as the "honorary provost." The costs of the common ridings, formerly borne by town councils, were paid by local "trusts" and "common good funds" which in some towns gathered their income from the rents of the town lands. The controversy over what to do about the commons in these cases was a major point of friction during the government reorganization of 1975. By the time of the 1977 and 1978 common ridings, the customs had fallen into place that continue to prevail, and the *Southern Reporter* articles once again refer to just the "provost" of each town rather than including the title of "honorary."

Incomers to Selkirk say that they are being accepted into the town. As evidence, they offer the fact that it is possible for them to ride horseback with the lifelong residents on Common Riding Day. Yet the riding itself does not allow these nontownsfolk entry into the mysteries and meanings that the ceremonies hold for the "true Souter." That is, incomers are allowed to walk *behind* the ordered processional formed by the bounded groups of guilds and societies, but they are not permitted to walk *with* any groups, and they walk without being given any membership status. The life of the town depends on maintaining the fixed positions of the ancient ways; the death of the town is always threatened in the persons of incomers and the presence of professionals and middle managers who cross the town's boundaries for work or recreation. But at the same time, the life of the town depends on the economic health offered by the incoming dollars. The town is caught in an ambiguous situation.

The town's death and life are not the only motifs featured in the symbolic ride. The commons might be equally interpreted as the symbolic edge of the local world, beyond which the young men and women have transformed themselves from local citizens into wandering pilgrims on the private entrepreneurial journey of capitalism. The representation of the "exiles" and "colonials" is a mixed image of being both socially dead to the town and at the same time being periodically resurrectable through intermittent returns. Social death to the town is, in pragmatic terms, regenerative in certain ways: It fuels the ideology of Protestant individualism that is pervasive at the surface of the town's life, economy, religion, and education; it creates capital in the form of returned money and investments; and it preserves the population balance that is necessary for the town to continue from generation to generation at the same size and shape it has had for a hundred years. This, again, is an ambiguous situation.

My assertion that the riding of the town's boundaries and the founding of its internal memberships are connected to the symbolization of death and that life is congruent with the writings by a number of anthropologists, historians, and those in religious studies who have addressed the question of boundaries in the construction of meanings and social and cultural categories. In addition, the symbolic connection of death and boundaries is confirmed by numerous anthropological analyses of nonindustrial societies. Leach suggests that "the spatial and temporal markers which actually serve as boundaries are themselves abnormal, timeless, ambiguous, at the edge, sacred" (Leach 1976:35; see also Barth 1969, Boon 1982, Cohen 1985a, 1985b). In using Leach's analysis, Cohen goes on to explain that "in this respect the boundary marks not only the precise division between categories or states of being; it is also the margin, the in-between, the liminal. It is, therefore, a dangerous place in which to be" (1985a:319).

In the outward drain of young people through emigration and the lure of personal gain, Selkirk faces the possibility of its own death. The commons and their periphery represent here the bounded space of the town and its organized opposition not only to assaults from the "encroaching aristocracy" but also to all that they represent in the power and the force of the encroaching outside world. The emigration or social death of young people is also signified here by the multifaceted representational characteristic of cultural systems that

Turner calls the "multiple referral of symbols," akin to "multi-vocality" (Turner 1969). The death of the person to the town is necessary for the individual to experience life in Protestant, modern, and capitalistic terms.

As the riders conclude their encirclement of the town commons, they return past the steep hill and into High Street again, ending at the market square, where they observe the ceremony of the casting of the flags. The symbols of life and death in the marking of boundaries are admittedly more subtle than the more overt statements made in the ceremonies directed toward honoring the war dead at memorials, yet they are powerful statements to the participants about the threatened death and prevailing life of the town itself. To the "stayers" who have remained year after year, the elaborate ceremonial ride is a processual metaphor addressing one of the seemingly unresolvable contradictions of the Protestant world, that of the imperative to seek one's fortune in the "outside" world, conflicting with the imperative to remain behind and be loyal to one's family and local community. In addition, there is the ambiguity created by the conflict of traditions and worlds between the old ways of the medieval burgh, with its strict internal divisions and its separateness from the world beyond, and the new ways of the industrial town, with its workers at mills and manufacturing companies. There is the conflict of the old residents with the new ones, beginning in the 1830s and continually challenging the traditional town to assimilate its "incomers."

Finale: The Casting of the Colours

The final scene in the set of unfolding performance sequences merging the symbolism of war death, social death, and boundary maintenance is that of the "casting of the colours." In this moving ceremony, the standard bearer of the royal burgh and of each of five men's ceremonial guilds in turn stands alone atop a specially constructed stage, or dais, assembled each year on High Street in the market square. Each casts in turn his flag in figure-eight motions above his head to the rhythms of the tune "Up wi' the Souters o' Selkirk," played over and over again by the silver band. At the end of the final casting, by the standard bearer of the ex-servicemen, the flag caster bows his British flag to the floor, and there is, in the words of a local brochure, a "two-minute silence and the lament for Flodden, `The Liltin'." The figure of Fletcher looms large here, at the end as at its beginning, first as the royal burgh standard bearer casts the burgh flag and then as each standard bearer of the men's associations casts his own standard in a "scythelike motion." The final image of the tableau is the figure of the lone soldier and the national emblem of the Union Jack, bowed in remembrance.

The cult of memory, which Ariès (1974) described for the individual dead in the cemeteries in the United States and northwest Europe, is seen here in a collective version. Instead of the individual's being remembered alone, those who have died in wars or been lost to empires are memorialized together through the layering of battle symbolism and the images of heroic death. Ariès notes that "today the cult of the dead is one of the forms of expressions of patriotism, thus in France the anniversary of the victorious conclusion of World War I is considered the feast day of dead soldiers" (Ariès 1974:75). The war dead are associated with the feast day or holy day on both sides of the Atlantic. In reference to the emergence of Memorial Day in the United States, Davies notes that "there was a stress on various anniversaries which became as sacrosanct as any holy days" (Davies 1955:217).

In the Selkirk ceremony of casting of the flags, we find the close association of national and town symbols with clusters of referents, in another example of objective generality. Durkheim called on the French familiarity with this close association of flag and country when he attempted to explain his understanding of totemic emblems: "The totem is the flag of the clan" (Durkheim 1947:120, quoted in Singer 1984:112). In other words, the totem, the flag, the statue, or other symbolic emblems are in fact representations of a reality that is called up from memory into behavior at the display of the emblem. In this way the display of the flags in the casting ceremony evokes the memory of the town and recreates a glorious past.

The first-time attendee at a common riding and even the recurrent visitor is surprised and amazed at the absolute silence of the crowd of thousands, including young children and babies, as they listen to "The Liltin'." As a local saying goes, "there is not a dry eye in the market square." The plaintive melody of "The Liltin'" and the recall in the observance of Flodden of the words "the Flo'ers o the Forest are a'Wede away," the recall of the memorials to war and death, the recall of the impressive figure of the standard bearer going around the commons on the ridge of the hill followed by four hundred riders, and the recall of the excitement as the riders gallop into the town—these images bring together the town's present and past and merge them into one. Death is overcome in the moment of memory, and the town is the victor in an ongoing war with the outside world.

In Summary: Death, Life, and Boundaries
in Sacred and Civic Space

A Protestant town in Scotland, where Protestantism has been the official religion for over four hundred years, annually calls out symbols and expressions that are infused with older religious, often Catholic, iconography and liturgy to create a ceremony celebrating essentially *civic* themes. The common riding makes a statement of civic presence, continuity, and the acceptance and interpretation of change. Its town citizens who were born on burgh soil and lived and died there are honored individually at their deaths in correct Protestant, individualized services. Its dead who died in war and who died to the town through emigration are honored collectively as the town honors itself in its ongoing struggle with the world beyond the boundaries. Just as the Catholic corporate body of church consists of individual "souls" and continues its vigil for them as a collective entity long after their death, so the corporate body consists of "citizens" who, as individuals, may choose to stay or to leave and, by doing either of these, affirms one of the essential features of town life. In order to continue its fight against change and to stay alive, the town itself must change; and one feature in this change process is the generation and constant reconstruction of its ceremonial life.

In memorializing Flodden and the war losses, Selkirk memorializes its losses in all the past battles with external controls; and in affirming honor, heroic death, and vigilance to protect its boundaries, Selkirk combines its themes of life with its themes of death and remembrance. Its symbols include a centuries-long combination and recombination of those from an older, Catholic, and medieval world with those from a modern, Protestant, secular, and civic one. In this combination of symbols and metaphors we find a visible expression of an ongoing, often invisible, reality—the continuous transformation of old into new worlds in which Western society is engaged. Within this larger process of transformation from the bounded world of town and church to the unbounded one of open spaces and the lure of the unfamiliar—and in Selkirk, these two worlds coexist side by side—there is a potential for that crucial transformation of the person as a locally based, fixed position into the person as a searching, individual pilgrim on life's outward journey. For the modern, Protestant, capitalist world to be born, this is a crucial transformation.

3

Scenes of Feast and Fair: Dinners, Balls, Concerts, Races, Contests, and Shows

The common riding is a serious performance and a crucial civic ritual, but it is also a festival enacting the important human behavior known as *play*. In times of play, people and groups withdraw temporarily from their positions in the fixed orderliness of everyday social structure and stand aside to laugh at themselves and the ordered world, to turn it upside down, to smear it with humor, and to relax it with reversals of the normal order of things. Victor Turner includes this time out of time and space in his definition of *liminality*, or the "antistructure" of human social life (Turner 1969). Within the liminal phase of ritual it is possible to transform the everyday into the extraordinary, to give expression to the outrageous and the creative, and to break rules that one would never break under regular conditions. As an expression of this transformation, shops and trades, including the mills, all close for a holiday, and so the workers have a day of leisure. One exception to the closing is, predictably, the pubs, which in contrast with the normal open hours in midday and evening, are open from early morning until late at night under special laws. Celebratory riders and walkers begin early to imbibe strong spirits, and by afternoon the atmosphere is festive indeed. There are horse races on Friday afternoon

at a racecourse used only on that one day a year and called the "Gala
Rig." Betting is orchestrated by bookies in temporary stalls, and
refreshments are sold from a tent. On Friday evening there is the Common Riding Ball in Victoria Hall, for which occasion all those who
have purchased tickets don their finest long dresses and rented dinner
suits and dance until the wee hours. All weekend there are "shows"—
a carnival in the park, rides, games, and merriment. Even on the Saturday following Common Riding Day, the play activities have not
yet ceased: A gymkhana is held at the rugby field, with athletic events,
foot races, and highland dancing contests. By Saturday night when
the locals gather at the various clubs for the final time of singing and
drinking, the end of the holiday is in sight; and by Sunday morning
the town is sound asleep.

When asked about the common riding, one of my local experts
answered my question "What are you doing here?" with his own version of liminality and antistructure:

> What we are doing here is we are having a wonderful time! It's like a
> fair or festival in olden times. Everyone relaxes and lets loose for one
> day. People who normally work in mills and shops ride horseback, play
> in the band, follow the foot processional, watch the flag casting, go to
> the races, drink and eat and celebrate in general with their friends and
> neighbors.

A Church of Scotland minister who is known to disapprove of
these excesses cynically says of the common riding that "it is just a
little town amusing itself." Another minister condemned more
harshly the suspension of rules and immersion in revelry by observ-
ing that "all the Border festivals are the same thing—they are pagan-
ism mixed with relics of the Roman Catholic saints' days. And they
are certainly *not* Protestant!" The common riding as play indeed
reverses the Protestantism and ethical morality of the bourgeousie.
It turns on its head the resentment of the aristocracy and privilege
and wealth by having a humble lad be the king for a day; it plays with
the fears and frustrations of structured inequality and laughs outright
at the deep cleavages in the social fabric so that its hidden injuries
might be temporarily repaired; it ceremonializes and sacralizes the
painful experience of untimely death in war and emigration but follows and encases this seriousness in the pure pleasures of ongoing
life as it can be found in simple enjoyments and excesses. And like
any elaborate performance or production, the common riding requires
months of planning.

Preparation and Production:
Backstage in the Making of Tradition

The activities preceding the actual common riding day are themselves elaborate and intricately orchestrated. Each event has a traditional slot in the calendar that unfolds throughout the spring. The first official event is the election of the royal burgh standard bearer by the committee known as the Common Riding Trust (a function performed by the burgh council before the reorganization of local government). The choice of the young man to carry the burgh flag is one that is itself carefully orchestrated through requirements not only to have been "born on the burgh soil" and be unmarried but also to have served as an attendant at previous common riding ceremonies. The standard bearer is announced in a ceremonial escorting through the town by the committee and ex–standard bearers and attendants, a process known as being "chaired out," meaning that the standard bearer is actually carried on a chair above the shoulders of the supporting young men in a processional around the town behind the silver band. In spring of 1986 this event took place on the last Friday in April and was reported as follows:

> The Selkirk Standard Bearer for 1986 is Ian Rodgerson, of 38 Murry Place. . . . The 25-year old TV engineer, who has already ridden the Marches 18 times, was chosen by Selkirk Common Riding Trust on Friday night from among 14 applicants for the post.
>
> He is the son and brother of previous Standard Bearers, and will have his younger brother Kevin as one of his attendants. . . .
>
> The formal part of Friday's ceremonies took place in the Town Hall, with the Common Riding Trust meeting at 6:35, and the Standard Bearer being chaired out for a procession round the centre of the town, behind the band, 25 minutes later. In between, there was time for memories, with chairman, Provost Tom Henderson presenting the John Pollock Bequest photograph to Ian's predecessor Tommy Renwick, and he was later to congratulate Elliot Grieve on his silver jubilee as an Ex–Standard Bearer, and note that Regional Councilor and former Provost, Len Thomson, was passing the half-century of the time he had cast the Flag of the Hammermen.
>
> The 1986 Standard Bearer was taken to the Victoria Hall where Ex–Standard Bearer Gordon Hislop promised him the support of his predecessors and the community. (*Southern Reporter*, May 1, 1986, p. 3)

The appointment of the standard bearer begins the formal sequence of pre-common riding events, although there is a great deal of informal activity at all times from one year to the next. In the early spring, men have begun to ready the racecourse, the "Gala Rig" for use on the common riding afternoon, mending fences and tracks and tending to the turf. As each group receives applications or considers the nominees for its own standard bearer, there is much informal discussion, serious talk in the men's drinking clubs and on the street, about who will be chosen for each one. And among the householders who have relatives in Canada and other overseas locales, there is a year-long correspondence and series of planning activities surrounding their possible presence or absence at common riding time.

The Victoria Hall has been reserved for the Common Riding Ball (almost automatically every year for the Friday evening after the first Monday in June), and the band engaged, the catering tent booked, and the same with all the necessary practical arrangements for the gymkhana and athletic games on the Saturday following. Every available hotel room and bed and breakfast is reserved for months in advance. Horses have been engaged or will be within weeks of the date itself, and proper riding attire is acquired or borrowed. Mothers and wives save household money to have extra and fancier-than-usual food and drink during the festive weekend and to buy new clothes for their children and themselves. One ad promoted "New Curtains for the Common Riding . . . Delivery guaranteed" (*Southern Reporter*, May 1, 1986). In the weeks before the event one finds merchants painting or festooning their storefronts, and employees of the local government cleaning and repairing with special care. On the days before, a dais or stage is constructed on the market square to be used for flag casting, which is then removed and reconstructed year after year. Ropes of colorful banners are hung from the light posts and across the streets from building to building.

Also behind the scenes and important to the staging of the performance, the rehearsals begin. The rehearsal for the flag casting takes place on evenings throughout May on the lawn of Wellwood, a council-owned old people's home converted from the former town house of a wealthy mill owner. On the Wellwood lawn each standard bearer of the guilds and the royal burgh standard bearer himself are instructed on the proper method for casting the flags, the choreography of the touching ceremony in which there will be no dry eyes in the audience if properly performed. There are special "casting flags" of lighter weight for easier movement, and there is a special way in which the flags must be hoisted and waved around the head in figure-eight circular motions to the rhythms of the band playing "Up wi' the Souters of Selkirk." Former standard bearers of guilds and of the burgh are on hand to instruct and lead in practice those neophytes who are like stage rookies, excited about being cast in the part but nervous lest they make a mistake.

The significance to the young man who serves as the royal burgh standard bearer is one of a strong sense of personal honor and responsibility. For the older men who have carried the flag, it has become the high point of their past lives and a point from which to count other events in time. One of these men, who carried the town flag in the 1940s, remarked that his father had begun to teach him the day he was born "all the things I would need to be standard bearer." This man reported with feeling that in his day "the standard bearer was a hero." He pointed out how expensive it is to be a standard bearer and that whereas when he was a boy the person chosen was always "from the manufacturing and business groups" [merchants, burgesses, owners of shops or commercial enterprises], nowadays they give a grant . . . and the neighbors take up a collection." The launching of a son into this position continues to require financial commitment by a whole family, however, and remains a position of local hero, in spite of the nostalgic report that things are not the same as they once were.

In the same conversation in which he bemoaned lost days of heroes, the ex–standard bearer to whom I spoke told of his own role in preparing the royal burgh standard bearer for 1978. He spent numerous Sundays at the home of another local worthy, instructing the newly chosen young man through informal means, describing what had to be done, "briefing" him, as the speaker put it, so that the young man would be able to carry out his duties properly.

There also are rehearsals for the horses and riders who have the leading roles. The central figures are eager not to make any miscalculations or to be unskilled in their techniques of horsemanship or public ceremonial manners. The standard bearer and his attendants practice the difficult places on the route, including the crossing of the river and the "galloping in at the toll" on horses they must learn to trust and be able to control. There are special "flag horses" for hire in Borders stables, horses that are such veterans of common ridings and of riding under the waving standards of the towns that they are not likely to be frightened by the movement of the flags, people, or other horses or the noise of the band. It is one of these horses that the standard bearer hopes to rent and to have as his ally for the most visible day in his life.

In addition to rehearsals for the horses and riders who are in principal positions, there are necessary precautions to be taken by the organizing committee to ensure the safety of all the riders and the orderly procession of horses, a procession that may range between four and five hundred in number from year to year. This is no small organizational task. The *Southern Reporter* printed one year this note on the plans:

> The Common Riding Trust held a final meeting to draw up plans for this year's Common Riding, last Wednesday.
> Forty-one stewards have been appointed, including six on foot. Some 12 of the mounted stewards are lady riders, and first-aid help will be widely available.
> A police radio link, along with walkie-talkies, will be in use on the hill. An inspection of the two river crossings will be held in the early morning of Common Riding day. (*Southern Reporter*, June 12, 1986, p. 4)

In 1987 high water ruled out crossing the Ettrick River. In other years, in other towns, the same precautionary rerouting was observed: One year, the Selkirk standard bearer was actually swept away and drowned during the Galashiels Brawlads Day ride out, in an attempt to cross the flood-swollen Tweed. Riders have been known to be thrown off their mounts; bones have been broken; and other injuries have been sustained over the years. A part of the lasting enjoyment of the ride is the telling and retelling of stories of bad weather and near-disasters on the ride and the relating of one's diligence in returning safely and with dignity.

During the week immediately before the common riding, every evening is scheduled with one or more dinners, concerts, or "bussin's" of the various societies. The *Southern Reporter* routinely devotes part of a page to the Common Riding Week to reports of these affairs and the official pictures taken of the dignitaries. Then, on the week following the common riding, it devotes an entire page to pictures of the event and another part or full page to stories about the events within the day's ride and its ceremonial surroundings. The double-page spread of newsprint and photographs presents an impressive window into the pageantry of the day and its surrounding and supporting gatherings and performances. Over the years the photos tend to take on a ritual placement in the spread of coverage: On the week of the common riding, on the left side of the double page one sees the formally posed pictures of the ex–standard bearers for the royal burgh who were at the "top table" at the dinner, usually those celebrating a special anniversary; the previous year's standard bearer; the current standard bearer; and the provost. One might also expect to find the formal picture of the top table guests for the United Crafts dinner, also featuring the provost along with the deacons and standard bearers for the hammermen and the weavers. There may or may not be pictures in this week or the next of the Incorporation of Fleshers' dinner or the dinner of the British Legion, but there are stories reporting these as well as the merchants' dinner. The formal pictures of the standard bearers with their "lady bussers" appear on the left side of the double page on the week reporting the common riding, along with a picture of the Colonial Society, often headed "The Exiles," seated in posed lines before their concert and bussin' on the Wednesday evening of Common Riding Week. The right side of the double page is filled with shots capturing the action and drama of the street processions, the crossing of the Ettrick, and other expected "scenes."

The layout of these photos in ritually repeated form from year to year complements the ritual formality of the events themselves, and the setting of "scenes" for photographers to capture adds to the continuation of these traditional scenes as essential to the unfolding process of the ritual walking, riding, and casting of flags that comprise the day. In its adherence to the orderly sequencing of protocol and to the appropriate scenes for photographs, the common riding has characteristics of a formal American wedding as staged in an etiquette-ruled segment of that society. In the photographing and reporting of both weddings and common ridings, the planners and the actors must cooperate with a protocol that they did not design but that they know must be followed in order for the event to be "right." And the reporters, photographers, caterers, florists, outfitters, and principals themselves have in their heads or in their instruction books for easy consultation just what the rules are that must be followed. So it is with the common riding and its public presentation afterward for saving and constructing "rightness" for future years.

On the week of common riding in 1990, the *Southern Reporter* carried this traditional report of the start of the festivities:

> Common Riding excitement built up this week at the annual round of dinners and bussin's.
>
> On Monday evening, the Selkirk Ex–Standard Bearers Annual Dinner took place in the Victoria Hall. Dumfriesshire MP Sir Hector Monro proposed the toast to the Royal and Ancient Burgh. And in his reply, Provost Tom Henderson paid tribute to Sir Hector's work in the aftermath of the Lockerbie disaster. . . . Provost Henderson also wished Harry Russell a "Hail Smilin Morn, Safe Oot, Safe In" on his Silver Jubilee as Royal Burgh Standard Bearer.
>
> Chairman, Ex–Standard Bearer Harvey Lockie proposed the toast to the Royal Burgh Standard Bearer, to which John Wilson replied.

Ex–Standard Bearer John Beveridge gave the vote of thanks after George
Miller toasted Selkirk Common Riding and Ex–Standard Bearer Elliot
Fraser replied. (*Southern Reporter*, June 12, 1990, p. 4)

The proposing of toasts and replies to each one is standard protocol at the dinners. These have carefully been written in advance
by those asked to propose and reply, and the subject is designated and
predictable: the toast to the Royal and Ancient Burgh and its reply,
the toast to those ex–standard bearers who are having anniversaries
and its reply, the toast to the current standard bearer, the toast to the
Selkirk Common Riding, and the vote of thanks. There is a kind of
liturgical quality to these events.

The flags are "bussed" one by one through the week, but the
burgh flag is not "bussed" until the morning of the ceremony, and
then it is done in special settings on the balcony of Victoria Hall for
the entire assembled town to witness as the provost charges the standard bearer with delivering the flag back "unsullied and untarnished"
and wishes him "Safe oot, safe in." In 1990 the order of the dinners
and "bussin's" was the following: Friday night, the United Crafts
dinner (weavers and hammermen); Saturday night, the Incorporation
of Fleshers' annual bussin; Monday evening, the Ex–Standard Bearers'
annual dinner; Tuesday evening, the Merchant Company bussin; and
Wednesday evening, the concert and bussin of the Colonial Society.
The British Legion also holds a dinner in the legion's club rooms. At
each of these dinners and public events, the provost and the royal
burgh standard bearer both appear. Each is invariably asked to propose one of the toasts or reply or to give the vote of thanks. It is an
exhausting week for the principals and their attendants, as well as
for their families and friends.

Following the flag casting at the close of the common riding itself,
yet another round of celebration and group-oriented drinking begins.
Known as "foys," the events following the solemn services resemble
the celebrations of soldiers after a battle or that of wedding guests
and newlyweds at the wedding reception. There is great gaiety and
singing, drinks and food, and overall revelry. While the official group
"foy" is being held for each men's society, there are numerous small
gatherings at local clubs, hotel bars, and private houses, with the same
people returning year after year to the same places at the same times
for the celebration and singing of the common riding songs.

In general, as soon as the flag casting is ended, the solemn part
of the ceremonies gives way to this celebratory atmosphere of feast
and fair. On the mill haugh the carnival shows are set up for the week,

and many of those who are not directly involved in the planning, riding, or racing spend their afternoon and evening in this festive way; others eat and drink together in the houses of friends or take walks to visit neighbors.

In the afternoon of Common Riding Day, the "Gala Rig" is the scene of the annual horse races. In Selkirk there are said to be "one hundred people who really do all the work for the common riding." These include the members of the Common Riding Trust, planners for each of the men's associations, those who serve as stewards and assistants on the ride, and members of the Race Committee. The Race Committee is responsible for keeping the racecourse in shape from year to year and making certain that on Common Riding afternoon it is in peak condition. On the Sunday before the common riding, known as "Show Sunday," the committee holds a gathering at the rig when all involved in the planning and staging can come up to the racecourse and look at the efforts of the committee's work.

By the afternoon of the Friday of the common riding, when the races begin, there is an atmosphere of gaiety in the air. There are special races for those horses who have gone around the boundaries and other races for horses who are racers only. Special trophies and prizes are awarded year after year. Horses race in each of the town's festivals and ridings, and so local and regional racers become known for their speed and stamina, and there are bets taken all around. A catering tent provides the food and drink.

On Friday evening those who have planned far in advance, booking their tickets and renting their formal attire, end the day at the Common Riding Ball in Victoria Hall. On one year in the late 1970s twelve hundred tickets were sold. The tickets always are limited in supply and assigned in priority to the principals, town dignitaries, planners of the common riding, and visitor principals from other towns and then are opened for sale to the public. The women dress formally in long gowns, and the men rent formal dinner suits (the American "tux").

The evening begins around 9:00 P.M. and lasts well into the early morning, ending with the "Standard Bearer's Reel" danced by the principals and their young women partners. In some of the other Border towns both a young man and a young woman are chosen by the town's committee to represent the town on its ride; in Selkirk only the man is chosen, and his "partner for the Common Riding Ball" is announced in the *Southern Reporter* in advance of the event. She does not accompany him on the ride or at other public functions as an official town figure. At the ball the standard bearer and his young lady are treated as visiting royalty would be treated, and they conform to the part, strolling about chatting with the guests and greeting the visitors from other towns. Many of the songs played by the band are traditional Scottish songs and the traditional dances are familiar to the attendees and greatly enjoyed by all. At the regular dances the young people hold periodically in the same hall throughout the year, one is more likely to find "disco dancing" or various popular kinds of dances to the music of traveling groups or disc jockeys booked for the occasion. For the Common Riding Ball, however, the age of the participants is older; the people are more likely to be town leaders; and so, the music played is in keeping with the tradition of the event.

On the Saturday following the riding of the common lands, the gymkhana and athletic games are held at Philliphaugh field and the cricket field. The gymkhana includes contests of skill on ponies (jumping, performing, and generally "showing" ponies); the games provide a format for contests among athletes in running, jumping, throwing the discus, and other set pieces of field and track skills. Some athletes travel about through the summer competing in these events, and some of them are well known to the audience. During the day there also are contests of children for Scottish country dancing and contests among pipers. The silver band sets itself up in concert style for the afternoon after a procession from the town at midday. Throughout the afternoon the sound of the band's music wafts across the field as the competition unfolds, and the spectators stroll about greeting one another and discussing the previous day: Was it a good common riding, which horses misbehaved, wasn't the weather glorious/horrible, and so forth. Visitors from overseas mix with their former friends and classmates; introductions are made for the incomers and ethnographers. Again, one finds the catering tent doing a strong business in both food and drink.

By Saturday evening even the most avid common riding fans are beginning to tire and slow down. As the final event of the weekend, each of the clubs holds on Saturday an evening of singing, dancing, and informal visiting for its members. In the club the voices ring out again with the common riding songs, and the hale and hearty atmosphere of the weekend is created one more time. On the following day, most of the people of the town are very tired indeed.

In listing and describing the events resembling the feast and the fair I have only touched on the actual, vast number of private and semiprivate parties, dinners, breakfasts, and get-togethers that are going on at all times over the Common Riding weekend, not to mention the buildup of various meetings, dinners and committees that precedes them. For those who are to ride, there is the ritual shampooing of the horses on the evening before the ride, and some braid the horses' manes or tie ribbons on them; for those who are to lead the procession or carry the town flag or be attendants, there are rehearsals, briefings, assembling of costumes, and then the appearance at all the public events; for the person in the street there are sessions of excited talk before the day and the preparation and feeding of family and visitors. Everyone is busy and excited. The town is changed on Common Riding Day; one ex–standard bearer declared "On Common Riding Day everything is different!" Another observed, "It's like magic on Common Riding morning with the flute band going round the town. The whole town is transformed." A third testified "There's Common Riding, . . . and then there's everything else."

Women and Men in the Making of the Common Riding

"Where are the women?" one might ask after reading this far into my ethnographic descriptions. The answer is that they are essential as actors, workers, designers, and stage managers of performance, to creating both the meaning and experience rendered symbolically here—the town as mother.

Woman as *symbol* encompasses all the interwoven representations of town-ness I have attempted to explore. The town is always spoken of as "she," as sometimes the sweetheart long lost to whom one returns and sometimes as the mother of the "sons and daughters of the burgh." She is represented in song as "the fairest of them all" and in ceremonial rhetoric as one who "embraces the returning colonials." The flag is assigned to be carried around the marches and returned "unsullied and untarnished," in a reference to the town's virtue and honor, jealously guarded from violation by those from "outside." And she is seen as the woman at Ladywood Edge weeping by the side of the road for her young men lost at Flodden.

Women as *actors* in common riding liturgy hold an ambiguous role in the performance. The real-life women of Selkirk may ride horseback in the procession if they choose to do so, or walk in the street processions, but they are not allowed in the segmented brotherhoods, the traditional guilds, behind the banners. Women may, however, walk with the Colonial Society, a modern-world guild with both men and women members. Women do not carry or cast the flags; instead, they perform the role of "lady busser" in tying on the ribbons.

Although they may not be standard bearers, they may and do in fact hold positions in the town offices and the elected representative offices of the district and regional councils. For example, the provost of Hawick is a woman. In her role as figurehead for the civitas, she takes a visible role in the common riding, handing over flags and making toasts and speeches, but she is not admitted to the all-male Callant's Club and its gathering at a lodge house known as the "hut" used during the riding of the commons. In Hawick, in contrast with the other burghs, women have not been allowed to ride in the horse procession at all. In Selkirk, women are on public and community committees involved in planning the civic event, and they are on the stage or at the top table at the dinners and bussin's, but a woman cannot be the royal burgh standard bearer.

The women's primary part in the production of the ritual drama is the one that is least visible, that of woman as *liturgist*.[1] In the elaborate staging and performance of this popular liturgy, women are like "stage managers" in the backstage arrangements for the common riding festivities. Mothers and wives buy and prepare food for parties and guests, buy and rent clothes for the riders and walkers in their families, and clean house and make ready for the overseas relatives. As the managers of their household budgets, all year long the women juggle daily requirements with the future demands of the common riding's special needs or wants. They also are the letter writers and card senders to overseas family members and are the hostesses who receive them when they return "from all over the world." And significantly for the overall understanding of the connections between symbol and experience, the women are the senders of their own sons and daughters to the far reaches of empire and the mothers who wait with open arms for the returned colonials.

In the worlds of modern and of traditional Scotland, women, like men, balance their modern position as citizens—a position of individuality and equal rights—with their traditional position as town and family member—a position of obligation with responsibilities to maintain the older, ascribed order of idealized past burgh life. Women, like men, are caught in the webs of meaning attendant to the changing worlds of mill work and work in microcomputer factories existing alongside the worlds of merchants, burgesses, trade guilds, childbearing, housekeeping, and common riding preparation. The ceremony creates an alternative time and place for these two worlds to exist side by side.[2]

II
THE TOWN

The town as a place and an idea is a key construct in Western culture. It stands for order, "community," belonging, and loyalty to home, kin, and country. Town symbolism includes a vast array of images and icons: the steeple of a courthouse or church; a square or wide main street; in the Catholic world, a patron saint; and in the Protestant world, a revered founder or hero. The town as an organizing social feature of human settlement falls conceptually between the "country" and the "city." It is "urban" in definition and "civic" in nature, yet it does not involve the scale of organization of city life or encompass the heterogeneous cultural segments of the metropolis or megalopolis. It is often thought of as "rural" or "provincial" and yet does not involve the sparsity of population or the agricultural economy of the countryside. The town is, in fact, a distinctive social form and symbolic entity. It is a nucleated settlement bounded by certain limits, incorporated or essentially functional as a corporate body that has its head in a council or other elected or appointed corporate representative body. It is composed of an orderly succession of generations arranged in a culturally defined social pattern, housed in culturally defined housing, and making a living in culturally defined ways of mercantile or manufacturing enterprises. And in its civic ritual, a town engages in the production and reproduction of its vision of itself year after year.

4

Selkirk the Town

Selkirk is most beautiful from Peebles Road, set far across the meadow on the other side of the River Ettrick, a silhouette of rooftops and spires on the hillside above the river valley below. This is especially true in late spring and early summer when the meadows are in bloom and the sun comes out for some midday hours, brightening up the cricket field and rugby fields just past Phillipaugh, the ancient farm on burgh lands. One crosses the river over the bridge that when first built in 1820 was called the New Bridge and has been called that over several reconstructions. On the Peebles Road side of the river lies Bannerfield, the sprawling housing estate built after World War II to shelter a growing population. Just beyond the river is the mill haugh, built up since the early 1800s with textile cloth–manufacturing facilities of various types and sizes, now mostly buildings taken over by other kinds of businesses or used for other functions. Newer metal buildings cover spaces now devoted to Selkirk's largest employer, Exacta Corporation, a maker of printed circuits for the computer industry, stretching along a road that was once the site of the "old toll." Tannery, building yard, and garage sit near the area known as the "Green." On a hill to the right at Heatherlie Park are two stately houses turned into hotels. Up the hillside into Selkirk one passes nineteenth-century additions to the town's housing from the heyday of the mills, to High Street, running along the hillside, where the market square is the center of commerce and general activity for the five thousand or so people who inhabit this small Border town. Facing the market square is the old court house where Sir Walter Scott once held sheriff's court for Selkirkshire; nearby is the Pantwell commemorating an early burgh water source and later engraved with a memorial for war dead. Signs direct the newcomer to Halliwell's Close, one of the few relics of medieval Selkirk to survive the nineteenth-century building boom. Inside in a former ironmonger's shop are the museum and visitor center. The old jail a block away is now the library; the burgh council buildings have been turned into the regional headquarters offices of several divisional administrations and for Radio Tweed; and Victoria Hall has had a face-lift; but essentially Selkirk remains the same as it was when I first saw it in 1972, and then it had been the same for almost a hundred years.

Selkirk as a Town Community

The Selkirk of today is a prosperous town, in the sense that any Scottish Border burgh is prosperous. The residents find work in the remaining woolen textile mill or at Exacta, in the locally owned shops and stores on High Street, in businesses that sell and repair autos or farm equipment or do construction. There also are local branches of the major banks and the savings and loans. Unemployment is low in the Border towns because everyone shares the jobs and the work, and in most families two or more adults each have at least part of a job, so that everyone is at work at least a part of every day.

In the Selkirk I first encountered in early 1970s, many of the town families had one or more adult workers who were employed in part-time positions in mills or shops. The older men and women had been made redundant or were collecting old-age pensions from the government, and the young and the skilled who had stayed in Selkirk were working for Exacta or were apprenticed to trades or textile-related specialties. Very few families had excess money. There were few cars in those days, and the majority of the houses in the town were owned by the council or absentee landlords. Everyone made maximum use of the back garden for vegetables, which then were traded with neighbors.

The daily shopping was done on High Street by calling at the butcher or fishmonger, the greengrocer, the baker, and the grocer. Two multifunction groceries were in operation, the Co-op and another "supermarket," but local housewives felt that the fresher and better goods were at the local specialty shops and that the profits of these would go into pockets of neighbors rather than strangers, and so these were the preferred vendors. In addition to butcher, baker, fishmonger, greengrocer, and grocer (multiples of each of these existed) on High Street could be found local chemists' shops, ironmongers, drapers, newsagents, stationers, confectioners, cafés, gift shops, and coffee shops. Morning shopping rounds were essentially an exercise in social networking. High Street was buzzing with movement and dotted with baby prams sitting outside each shop with their tiny passengers waiting patiently while mum shopped and exchanged news. In these times of relatively scarce funds and small disposable incomes, the commodity of time became valuable. The economic relations, as in the non-money economies of noncapitalist worlds, were deeply embedded in personal relations, and the sharing of time, energy, goods, and services along lines of friendship and kinship became essential to the ongoing support of the town's social and financial universe.

As economic times improved over the years and new industries came to the Borders, more evidence of a money economy began to surface: people driving into another town for shopping at megashops, especially in Edinburgh or Carlisle; people ordering goods from catalogs; people who could not previously afford to own a car owning one; the addition of refrigerators, washers, televisions, and videocassette recorders to homes previously without them or previously making do with minimal equipment.

The Borders has been, since the early 1800s, an almost one-industry region, with the heavy concentration of woolen textile mills and related companies ruling the economic scene. For Selkirk, the turn into textile manufacturing came with the building of the road from Galashiels in 1833; the nineteenth century also saw the growth of Selkirk from a small commercial burgh into a large industrial town. Mills lined the haugh of the Ettrick, and the lads and lasses of the former countryside turned into workers in the mill floor, governed by the factory time clock and the whirr of the looms. Like all one-industry towns and regions everywhere, Selkirk and the Borders have suffered from the cycles of boom and bust that govern woolen textile prices. In good times, the fully employed town has been prosperous, and the merchants and tradespeople have adopted the money economy of modern capitalist consumption. In bad times the under-employed population has turned to barter and shared resources. Excess workers have left for colonial destinations in Canada, Australia, and New Zealand where there is prosperity in the woolen trade or other urban employment.

The Borders today is a region that continues to be famous for its high-quality woolen goods, and the luxury shops and stores of London and New York continue to feature Scottish woolens at luxury prices. Competition from synthetics and cheaper manufacturers in other locales, however, have driven many of the woolen manufacturers out of business and left their facilities either empty or reinhabited by firms in other kinds of business or manufacture.

In Selkirk in the 1980s the largest employer was Exacta Corporation, maker of electronic components. Another, newer industry is Selkirk Glass, which in 1990 opened an enlarged showroom for its line of fine hand-blown paperweights. In June 1990 it was announced that the old river haugh would be the site of a regional shopping mall to house one megashop and several medium-sized shops. The shopping mall would, of course, change the face of buying in Selkirk and surrounding towns and affect the shops in High Street. The presence of this modern innovation echoes the introduction of centralized buying locations in Europe and the United States and signals yet another turn in the economic fortunes of the "auld toon."

Selkirk has experienced at least three economic phases over its hundreds of years as a town. The first one was the phase of royal burgh, franchised by the king to collect tolls and hold fairs, an economic arrangement including the town burgesses owning the commons and collecting rents as well as using the commons for their animals and crops. The medieval town shifted into an industrialized one at the onset of woolen textile manufacturing in the 1830s. The third economic phase can be seen in the demise of the mills as the single industry and the creation of a diversified local economic picture, along with an outward movement of working people into British cities and colonial locales.[1]

Whatever else the common riding is in terms of ritual and performance, it is certainly a means of marshaling and redistributing the local money capital and the symbolic capital. Horses are rented from Borders stables for hundreds of riders; ceremonial garb is rented or purchased for the principal riders in each town; dinners are catered at local hotels for each of the men's associations; concerts are staged at Victoria Hall; and drinks are bought all around repeatedly at the hotel bars and the mens' drinking clubs for weeks before and after the common riding and in great intensity on the weekend itself. The racecourse is readied and horses are matched; bookies set up stalls and collect bets. New clothes are added to each person's wardrobe for the ball or other events; the ball itself charges admission and provides catering and a bar plus an orchestra and the rent of Victoria Hall; and the gymkhana and athletic contests on the Saturday draw contestants from throughout the region to compete, eat Selkirk food, and fill their tanks with gasoline before returning home. Essentially, the common riding as an economic event is a classic combination of the centralization of personal capital and its redistribution within a local area, in which the ceremony of the exchanges is as important as their monetary value. The presentation of the gifts, for instance, to each standard bearer in the Border towns is a carefully orchestrated event, and the gift itself is chosen with care and surrounded with dignified toasts and speeches. The gift must be just right—not too expensive or too cheap, it must symbolize the event itself, it must be lasting, and it must represent a traditional theme. Each household provisions itself for a weekend of celebration and a possible influx of visitors. The hotels and bed-and-breakfast establishments are fully booked. A happy and successful common riding is truly an affirmation of the local world and its centrality in the ongoing economy as well as in every other aspect of its symbolic centrality.

The local economy has been boosted in recent years by the location in Selkirk of the district offices of the Borders Regional Museum and the regional headquarters of the Borders Regional Tourist Authority and the Borders Regional Library, the library offices and warehouses contained in the old St. Mary's Mill buildings by the river. These government operations are staffed in large part by people who live in other Border towns, part of the growing class of middle managers and professional government employees who cross the boundaries between towns in a process of transburgh travel that one elderly observer calls "Texanization."

Some of the Border spinning and weaving companies run buses or vans between the towns to ferry employees, especially if a company has consolidated in recent months or years, and some residents travel by bus to work in Galashiels, a nearby town of over ten thousand with wider job possibilities. Historically, Selkirk people worked in Selkirk, primarily in the woolen textile industry or the local commerce and crafts that supported the town's life.

Those residents who have lived all their lives in Selkirk prefer not to drive to other towns for work. Rather, newcomers, known locally as "incomers," are those most likely to drive across boundaries from town to town to work in district or regional offices, to hold supervisory or management jobs in mills in other woolen manufacturing towns, or to attend concerts or plays in other towns or even Edinburgh.

I sense that there are essentially two socioeconomic and symbolic groups of Selkirk inhabitants: One group is the "drivers," those who drive cars and cross between the towns for business or pleasure, and the other is the "walkers," those who prefer the immediacy of the town's streets and shops and whose life-style as mill workers and tradespeople suits them best for staying in Selkirk for most of their lives. The only regularized crisscrossing of border boundaries for these longtime local residents comes when visiting other towns for preset athletic events, especially in rugby competitions among the towns and, in the summer, for festivals and common ridings. Because of my own dislike of driving—even in America on the right side of the road and particularly in Britain on the left—I became part of the "walking Selkirk." In the mile walk down from Shawmount cottage in the mornings I became closely attuned to sheep and sheepdogs at their work, to neighbors digging in their gardens or hanging out their wash, and to the busy hubub of the street, where each shop and its queue for meat or vegetables or bread led to another chat with other Selkirk residents out for their morning rounds.

Because his work demanded more trips to other towns and because he does like to drive, my husband joined the "driving Selkirk" and became accustomed to the location and verbal exchange of the gas stations, the spots of lovely scenery in the valleys, and the roads and streets of other nearby towns.

The difference in these two ways of seeing is reflected in the evolution of our two perspectives. I found that I had a sense of Selkirk as being "far" from Melrose and Galashiels—and it seemed so if I wanted to get to these places on the bus—whereas my husband's driving viewpoint caused him to see Galashiels as nearby, Melrose as just up the road, and even Hawick as an easy ride, which to me was a distant eighteen miles away! Men and women of the mills and shops who comprise the walking Selkirk are the ones who are seen in highly visible roles in the common riding and in the multiple invisible roles of the informal leadership that has grown up after the disappearance of the burgh as a local authority.

The recreational world of the townsfolk creates a world separate from that of the surrounding countryside. In the towns a myriad of organizations and activities compete for the residents' leisure time—clubs; church societies; special-interest groups; teams for football, rugby, cricket, and bowling; and numerous civic committees and causes. In the weekly newspaper serving the Borders, the *Southern Reporter*, a special section called "Southern Noticeboard" lists activities under various categories. "This Week" begins with a list of organizations and events including the amateur operatic society and community drama association, concerts, annual dinners of lodges and men's organizations, squash matches, BMX club, youth club football, badminton, pool, darts, draughts, dominoes, chess, political associations, camera club, and church councils. It goes on to list "Law Courts" (a schedule of the sheriff's courts in Jedburgh, Selkirk, and Peebles), and then "Local Authorities," including Borders Local Health Council meetings, Roxburgh District Liscensing Board, Borders Regional Council, and, in one week checked at random, seven other civil committees and "authorities." In the same special two-column space are listed "Sporting Fixtures" such as rugby, football, and hockey.

In the fall and winter a separate heading appears, "Border Hunts," which tells the times and places of meeting for the favorite sport of the country gentry—fox hunting behind the hounds. Those who take part in this sport are set apart by owning horses and riding regalia and possessing the skill of expert horsemanship. Each hunt is organized as its own separate exclusive grouping: the Jedforest, Buccleuch, and Lauderdale, each following its own pack of hounds and having its own social events and "hunt balls" during the season. The country gentry also enjoy other horse-related sports and contests, which causes the townspeople to refer to their rural neighbors as the "horsey set." These horse owners sometimes ride in summer in the common riding's horse processions, but they are not a part of the town's life.

In contrast with the horse-owning set, the local residents who are chosen for figurehead positions in the common riding or who decide to ride in the processional as participants in the cavalcade must rent a horse for the occasion. Border stables keep a reserve of rental horses for the summertime cycle, so that one often sees the same horses over and over at the events. If there were a contest to determine the longest-tenured followers of the burgh flags, the winners would be these "common riding horses" that have been important figures for their entire lives. A significant aspect of all the Border ridings is the pageantry of the horse, the gallant and godlike figure that emerges when a human being mounts a horse, made more spectacular by the processing of hundreds of mounted riders over hills and across treeless moorlands. It is an image that has been prominent in Western visual representation since Greek and Roman times and one that today overlays the picture of the gentry at the hunt with that of the knight in full regalia, that of the Border reivers, and that of the vigilant burleymen riding the boundaries of the burgh lands.

The pageantry of the horse that plays such a large part of common ridings, with its accompanying inversions of orderly everyday burgh life into a world of carnival-like excesses of drama and feasting, is often disdained by the local clergy as an example of behavior in its most non-Protestant extremes. One Selkirk minister described the common riding as essentially a Catholic, if not pre-Christian, ritual that he would just as soon see disappear entirely from the calendar of burgh life. His distaste for a display of such proportions is not surprising when one considers the puritanical and austere requirements laid down in the Scottish Reformation and its resulting daughter church, the Church of Scotland. Selkirk and the Borders are heirs to this reform movement that attempted to scrub preexisting Catholic forms out of local church order and practice. Even the dour reformer son-in-law of John Knox himself was a parish minister in the local kirk for many years.

Selkirk's old parish kirk now stands in ruins next to its ancient cemetery just a few blocks from the market square on a road called Kirk Wynd. It was here that the Reformed Protestants laid down their rules and laws and also where the guilds and craft brotherhoods sat together under their banners for hundreds of years. In the booming mid-1800s, new church buildings were constructed; splinter churches formed representing various factions of the Church of Scotland; and congregations were started of the Anglican and Congregationalist denominations. The trend in the 1980s has been for the segmented and shrinking Church of Scotland's congregations to reunite and to combine congregations in an effort to economize. On a Sunday morning none of the local church buildings is even close to full of worshipers. Yet everyone is affiliated, most with the churches of their birth.

Politically, the towns of the Borders are not locally governing entities but fall into districts and regions administered under a plan instigated by Parliament in 1975 known as the "regionalization" of local governments. The dissolution of the burgh as a local governing body has been a major blow to local autonomy in the towns of the Borders, especially in the proud old royal burghs. Selkirk is in the Ettrick and Lauderdale District, along with its neighbor and rival Galashiels, several other towns smaller than these towns, and the small villages of the Ettrick valley. Within the Borders region are two other districts, Roxburgh and Peebles. The offices of region and district administrative units have been spread around the towns in order to attempt some sort of equity, but disagreement about situating offices and about the dominance of political control is continual. The councillors elected from Selkirk to the district and regional councils overlap in membership with that of the town councils before regionalization, just as the town councils of the reformed burghs after 1833 overlapped in membership with lists of the burgesses of past time.

The Border hills, with Selkirk in the distance. *(Photo by Jack Hunnicutt.)*

Provost hands over the burgh flag. (*Photographs of the 1985 Common Riding are courtesy of* The Southern Reporter *newspaper, High Street, Selkirk.*)

The cavalcade begins.

The royal burgh standard bearer.

The horses cross the Ettrick River.

The street procession.

The casting of the flags.

The royal burgh standard bearer casts the burgh flag.

In the early years after regionalization, one of the main points of contention with distant governmental power was the confusion over where the symbols of burgh authority—the provost's robes and chains and the local, historically significant relics—should be housed and whether to allow a ceremonial provost to appear in robes at the common ridings. Parliamentary planning soon lost out in this symbolic battle, and today, after the reestablishment of local presence throughout a fifteen-year span, each of the towns keeps its own ceremonial paraphenalia and brings it out in all its splendor at ceremonial times. With no local provost and no local council, the authority and presence of the towns have passed into the hands of an informal set of leaders, sometimes represented on the official district and regional council and sometimes serving in unofficial advisory capacities in informal conferences as needed. The local body responsible for staging the annual town ceremony in Selkirk is known as the Common Riding Trust. There is one elected local body called officially the "Community Council" in each town; in Selkirk it has been renamed as a statement: The Community Council of the Royal and Ancient Burgh.

The status of royal burgh assigned by the king in the twelfth century is an important one for Selkirk, as it looks backward at its history, one that sets it apart from that of the surrounding burghs—for instance, from Galashiels (a "burgh of barony") and Kelso (an ecclesiastical burgh tied to the abbey with the same name). Peebles, Hawick, and Selkirk had privileged positions from their establishment with this status, originally governed individually by their own burgesses who answered directly to the king and who had the right to collect tolls and taxes within their private domain. They also were given ownership of town common lands to be used by the burgesses for grazing their livestock. The burghs, in other words, were—from the time of their creation beginning in the early 1100s by King David I —little islands of civic government and economic independence. They were a result of the outreach by David and other early Norman kings of Scotland to spread the control of the nation into the hinterlands south of Edinburgh and to create loyalties in little ministate territories within the vast landholdings that surrounded the burghs. The king had also to keep these landholdings under his power and allegiance through the control of the landholding families. The establishment of the feudal system and the creation of dukedoms were essentially part of the same process of Scotland's royal assertion of control, as was the implanting of the great Border abbeys of Kelso, Dryburgh, and Melrose, as well as one near Selkirk that later moved.

The location of Selkirk as the site of a royal burgh in the twelfth century was connected to its strategic location near a favorite hunting castle of the Scottish king in the Ettrick Forest. Selkirk is said to have been "already an auld toun" in the 1100s when it gained its burgh status—probably it was really an "auld village" or castle hamlet. Historians of the period and the region are now certain that Selkirk adjoined a king's hunting lodge or "castle" and that it is one of the oldest of the Border towns to have gained this favored placement. Selkirk's history unfolds with several stages of change and realignment of people and conditions. Yet essentially from its foundation charters to about 1830, Selkirk changed little and remained a medieval-style burgh composed of burgesses, tradespeople, and craftsmen, of whom a few of the "burgh law men" (later shortened to burleymen), rode annually around the boundaries of the common lands to make sure that the marking stones had not been moved by any of the landowning families or the newly emerging nobility and aristocracy.

The structure of relationship of the burghs to the barons and aristocrats all over the Borders was essentially the same as that of Selkirk: dots of incorporated, independent, political and economic entities amid oceans of moorlands owned by clusters of, first, kinsmen and, later, lords and dukes. There were few roads before the nineteenth century, and therefore each town and its folk remained separate in crucial ways except for the intermittent instrusions of being marshaled out for battles with England and, later, with enemies of the British Empire. The representatives of the Crown in each county, or shire, were the appointed officials known as sheriffs, whose responsibility it was to see that the interest of the Crown were protected and that national laws were obeyed. This also included in the royal hunting preserve the policing of the royal hunting demesnes against poachers and the holding of sheriff's courts to ensure a modicum of law and order in the countryside.

The shape of the town is related to its past. At first, Selkirk was a small village, a mere crossing of two roads and a wide place where a market was held near the castle of the royal hunting preserve. Later the market moved down to the present site, which was more level, and gradually a triangular settlement of tradespeople and crafts grew up in conjunction with the castle (see Figure 10). The old maps of medieval Selkirk indicate that this pattern persisted through many centuries, until the early nineteenth century, in fact, when the addition of new housing for incoming mill employees from the surrounding valleys swelled the population to its all-time high. The shape of the town, however, has remained a variation on the old triangular pattern, with the "new town" running up the hillside and down toward the mill haugh (see Figure 11). It is the boundaries of the old town that are walked by the revelers on the Thursday night before the riding of the commons, and the opening words of the bailie are cried at each of the spots where once a "port" or gateway to the burgh stood in the past.

The common lands were an important feature of the shape of the burgh in the original charters and became a significant feature on the burgh landscape. Over the years the arguments over the commons have been one indicator of the structural differences between the world of burgh and the world of surrounding lairds and dukes. In the early years of Selkirk's charters—the twelfth to the sixteenth and seventeenth centuries—numerous disputes over town boundaries and rights to grazing the commons provoked confrontations with heads of the Kers, Murrays, and the lairds of Greenhead, Bridgelands, and other properties adjacent to the town's lands. Over the years, various councils of royal burghs settled disputes with local landowners, and the town commons shrank accordingly. The holdings were diminished even further as some land was sold off for use as farms and industries, until the commons owned by the burgh at the time of regionalization was a mere fraction of its original acreage. The final political and legal battle over the commons was fought over who should have ownership of common lands belonging to the burghs (including the right to collect rents) following the dissolution of the incorporations in 1975 through regionalization. The resulting agreement produced in each burgh owning common land a special fund known as the "Common Good Fund." The proceeds from renting the farmlands formerly owned by the burghs go into this fund, to be used for local improvement and, in the case of the Borders, for holding town festivals and common riding celebrations.

Today the town of Selkirk remains surrounded by holdings by large owners, whose world is one that remains separate in many ways from the world of the town. The primary landowner is the duke of Buccleuch. The farmers who own their own farms or who hold long-term leases from the Buccleuch estate operate fully modern food-producing organizations run as efficiently as any company, with the assistance of hired tractormen, shepherds, and laborers. The farmers often have been in the same farms for generations, and the workers are Borderers whose lives may have been spent on several farms in succession, living in the farm cottages or shepherds' cottages and moving only rarely.

The children of the farmers and the shepherds and tractormen all go to the local school. As a rule, the children of farmers marry those of other landowners or owners of shops or businesses; the children of farm workers marry the children of mill employees and employees in shops and stores. And in the circle of landed gentries of the dukes and earls—headed by the dukes of Buccleugh and Roxburgh—the children are sent away to private school and then to university, where they meet and marry one another's children or the children of other titled or moneyed persons from outside the Borders.

The people who became mill workers in the migration into the towns in the early 1800s were essentially people who had come in from the hills and valleys, where the mechanization of farming and the replacement of labor-intensive farming with herds of Cheviot sheep were displacing countryfolk and turning them from a rural landless working class into a town-based industrial one. Meanwhile, the same processes were making the landholders into more and more distant elites whose worlds faced increasingly toward Edinburgh and London.

Land, landownership, and all that they stood for have continued to be a major emblem of position and pride in British society until the present day. According to David Cannadine, the landowners of the late nineteenth century remained rulers of little principalities, whose domination was felt in their local domains and far outward into the halls of Parliament and the corridors of capitalism. He paints the following picture of the dukes and earls of 1888:

> The seventh duke of Devonshire once admitted that he had more houses than he knew what to do with. . . . But even he was outdone by sixth duke of Buccleuch, who boasted six houses in Scotland and as many again in England. In one year alone, 1888, the Buccleuch estates in Scotland provided 7,726 grouse, 1,121 black game, 2,342 partridge, 2,961 pheasant, and 3,639 hare, which were either consumed by the family and their guests, or given away. (Cannadine 1980:22)

In comparing the landholdings of these two dukes, Devonshire and Buccleuch, Cannadine finds the duke of Buccleuch, again, to outstrip the duke of Devonshire. He notes that by 1883 the duke of Devonshire "was now possessed of estates in 11 English and three Irish counties." Cannadine goes on to say, "If he had been a grandee of substance before, he was now one of the great subjects of the crown, with an acreage only surpassed by Scottish magnates like the dukes of Buccleuch and Sutherland" (1980: 22). From late nineteenth-century computations made by Bateman, Cannadine lists the duke of Devonshire's estates in 1883 as 198,572 acres. And so the duke of

Buccleuch held a vast acreage indeed! The major difference, of course, was that the Scottish dukes held their lands in open moor and heath, ill suited for agriculture and remote from towns of any size or industrial development potential. Their hope of capitalizing lay solely in the removal of tenants and the introduction of Cheviot sheep.

Historian G. E. Mingay (1963) focuses on the eighteenth century as the crucial time for the amassing of large estates and landholdings throughout Britain and the accompanying consolidation of power in the hands of the landed class. The "land improvement schemes" of the dukes in the eighteenth and early nineteenth centuries were the root of two major shifts on the Scottish landscape. One was the creation of the "new towns" or industrial developments in the central belt of Scotland near the new manufacturing sites, and the second was the removal of vast hordes of Scots people outward into the colonial world.

The new towns being formed in the Borders were most often adjacent to existing older villages or "farmtouns," as in Langholm with New Langholm in 1778, and in Galashiels between 1770 and 1790 at the onset of the textile mills. Newcastleton is one example of a totally new town in this time period, developed by the duke of Buccleuch in 1793 to provide housing and mining work for his farm workers deposed to make way for the commercial production of sheep (Smout 1970:103–6). Smout attributes the small number of eighteenth century planned towns and villages in the Southeast, especially the Borders, to the fact that "there were already enough large villages. The Anglian nucleated settlements did not need rebuilding on a different ground-plan, and late medieval or seventeenth century burghs of barony, . . . were numerous and well established" (1970:106). These burghs of barony include both Langholm and Galashiels, to which the "new town" for mill workers could be annexed. The earlier royal burghs of Selkirk and Peebles had been established by the kings for some of the same reasons, consolidation of power and commerce. In these burghs as well, the "new towns" could adjoin the old. Evidence of this can be found in the changing shape of Selkirk over the years, as demonstrated in the maps in Figures 10 and 11.

Smout describes the relation of the rural landowners to the new, planned villages and towns as one of continuing control. He observes that the landowners' description of the process of change called on the vocabulary of "modernization," "going to more effective farming methods' and similar kinds of conceptualizations." He sees the landowners as "sincerely paternalistic . . . treasuring the old values that a laird's worth was still to be measured as much by the abundance of the dependent population around him as by the weight of his rent roll" (Smout 1970:75).

It is significant that in Langholm, in one of the oldest and most traditional common ridings in the Borders, the ceremonial reference is to the original feus of the earl of Nithsdale in 1628, giving the Langholm dwellers the right to their common lands and the right to cut peat on the turf of the earl of Nithsdale's peatlaw. There is also reference to their right to hold a fair "by right and lot." There is no mention of the addition of the new town by the duke of Buccleuch except references to Langholm as the "auld toon." Today in Langholm's two-hundred-year-old "new town," houses are still held on long-term feus (some with one-hundred-year leases) from the duke and his managers. In Selkirk, until recent years, the royal burgh standard bearer was required to have been born not only "on the burgh soil" but also within the walls of "the auld toun," referring to the preindustrial Selkirk.

The meaning of the "landed class" in Britain is immensely complicated. One scholar, Norman Gash, writes of the social clout and the prestige positions accorded to landholding in the traditional governing elite in the mid-nineteenth century (his estimate is about four thousand families in 1815):

> Since 1688 they had dominated the political life of the kingdom. They controlled the electoral system, filled the benches in both houses of parliament, supplied the bulk of the clergy of the Church of England, the officer corps of the army and navy and the upper ranks of the diplomatic service. They commanded the militia; with the clergy they monopolized the magistracy; and through grand juries and quarter sessions they governed the countryside. Oxford and Cambridge had become finishing schools for their sons; contemporary painting and architecture reflected their aspirations and pursuits. They were conventionally regarded as, and to some extent actually were, a closely knit caste, and perhaps tended to be more so as the century wore on. The obvious distinction of hereditary title, including beside the peerage proper, the baronetcy, was underpinned by an elaborate legal system of entail, settlement, and primogeniture, designed to preserve and transmit the integrity of the estates from which they derived their status. Not land, but . . . land in the possession of families was the essence of the landed interest. (Gash 1979:18–19)

Under these conditions, it is no wonder that the townspeople of Selkirk were continuously vigilant over the ownership of their town's common lands. In its proprietorship of land, the town as an owning entity took on the social role of a landowning family and so had to be dealt with by the families as such. In other words, the town as a corporate owner was, as was the duke, a representative of a corporate "estate" and so had to be treated by the dukes and earls as an entity that is to be reckoned with as either collaborator or adversary. It is not surprising that the dukes and the surrounding families of Ker, Murray, and others waged a transgenerational battle with the burgesses over boundary stones, the use of grazing rights, and, later, the purchase of town lands for mill sites and country houses. It is also not surprising that these surrounding landholders have a history of attempting to control the council of burgesses, later the town councils, and, in the present day perhaps, the district and regional councils in order to press their advantage. In the Burgh Reform Act of 1833 and in the various acts of reform for burghs and churches, the hold of these powerful families has been lessened. However, even today the duke of Buccleuch holds vast expanses of land between Edinburgh and the Cheviot Hills, and the towns whose corporate limits border on these lands are the towns holding common ridings.

The Idea of the Town: History and Ethnology

The town of Selkirk and the other burghs of the Scottish Borders fit into an overall pattern of town making that has a history at least as old as those of the empires of the Middle East and Greece and Rome. It is a history in which the foundation of a town is connected to the foundation of a colony, with a military or administrative head as founder and a population of former villages incorporated into a space enclosed by walls, barricades, or, at the very least, "town limits" or boundaries. The formation of towns was one of the key ways that the Greeks expanded their control in the Mediterranean and the Romans extended their dominance northward in their years of empire in Europe and Britain (see Rykwert 1988).

In the case of Scotland there were no Roman implantations of towns north of Berwick, and Scotland was essentially a territory of scattered, kin-based affiliations of leaders who remained in a sort of "tribal hegemony" of power until the Norman kings came to power in Scotland. Smout dates the beginning of medieval society in Scotland to the eleventh century with the coming to the throne of Malcolm Canmore (1057–93), which began a change of influence, Smout explains, from Celtic-Irish to Anglo-Norman and later a "creeping influence of France and the Continent" (Smout 1969:20). Smout attributes the formation of the burghs to an effort at centralized con-

trol by Malcolm's sons, especially David I (1124–53), the founder of
Selkirk, who had spent forty years at the Anglo-Norman court in the
South of England. Smout points to four "tools" of kingdom making.

> Since Normans everywhere were the inheritors of Rome and the Euro-
> pean tradition, it is not surprising that the kings should work to give
> their polyglot kingdom a structure that would tend both to impose
> uniformity within and to be in harmony with contemporary ideas with-
> out. The tools they used were four—the introduction of feudalism, the
> reform of the church, the plantation of burghs and effective personal
> control over the machinery of government. (Smout 1969:22)

The four tools of creating a modern nation out of Scotland, a
former patchwork of Celtic kin groups, were interrelated, and all of
them affected the Borders in the twelfth century. First, the introduction of feudalism imposed territorial units that had nothing to do with
kinship, according to Smout's analysis; instead, all land was royal
land, and all authority resided in the king. In the Borders this control
was difficult to bring about owing to its remoteness from the centers
of power, and Smout concedes that even in the late Middle Ages, kinship was the dominating organizational feature of the countryside.
"In the rural Lowlands, people coagulated round the barons for secu-
rity, the barons coagulated into bands around each other" (1969:22).

> The further the baronies lay from the centre, the stronger would be local
> allegiance to the barons and the weaker the allegiance to the king. By
> the time the Borders were reached little allegiance was possible except
> to the Humes, the Armstrongs, the Scotts, the Chisholms and other
> great families who ruled in contempt of the central authorities except
> where it suited their book to give a show of loyalty to the king. . . . So
> outrageous was their disregard for royal law, and so pressing the need
> of the population for protection both from the English and other neigh-
> boring barons that the Borders came to form a zone almost as clearly
> defined and separate from the rest of the country in the late middle
> ages as the Highlands themselves. (Smout 1969:34)

This emphasis on respect for kinship and the pride in "good blood"
were, in Smout's view, a legacy of Celtic influence that gave Scotland an air of "uncouthness" to the world outside. Its pride in "blood"
contrasted and today contrasts decidedly with the pride in "law" held
by the Anglo-Norman citizenry of the royally constructed burghs.

The second interrelated action of the kings in their efforts at
unification and control was the reform of the church. In this endeavor
David I established organized dioceses made up of parishes, creating
a network of communication linking church government with royal

government and feudal arrangements. At the same time he instigated the establishment of abbeys throughout Scotland, including the abbeys of the Borders: Dryburgh, Melrose, Coldingham, and Kelso. David admired St. Bernard of Clairvaux, and he encouraged Cistercian and Tironian monasteries to be built at Melrose and Selkirk in this tradition, emphasizing hard work and withdrawal from the world. The monks in the Border abbeys were sheep farmers on what Smout describes as "an unprecedented scale," and "Cistercian Newbattle led the way in coal-mining and lead-mining" (1969:26). In addition to their industry and economy, the monasteries became models of literacy and intellectual life in a countryside previously unacquainted with them. As the Scottish church became stronger and more centralized, it, significantly, became increasingly distinctive from the church in England. In 1192 the pope established it as separate, "subject only to Rome" (Smout 1969:26).

The foundation of the burghs fit into these other royal initiatives. In the burghs as royal territories, merchants and tradesmen had specific rights. Immigrant skilled craftspeople were encouraged by the king to enhance their commercial ability and craft skills. "The people within the burghs," says Smout, "were never predominantly Celtic or Gaelic-speaking." Instead, "their main tongue was a dialect of English" (Smout 1969:28). Lists of burgesses from this time period include the names of Flemings, Normans, Angles, Scandinavians; the language now known as "old Scots" gives clues to the predominance of Angles and Scandinavians.

Finally, in the eleventh and twelfth centuries, the kings advanced their causes of social change through their own tight control and its institutionalization in the machinery of administrative units—sheriff-doms, or shires, each with its central point a royal castle or office where a court was held "in the king's name." The sheriff, as noted earlier, was also responsible for collecting rents from the vassals of the countryside and for raising an army for the king when required to defend Scotland against its English neighbor to the South. The Borders were crucial in this defense, and the history of the towns is entwined with the various skirmishes, raids, and outright wars that took place on Border soil. The most often woven into the song and story of today's civic ceremonialism is the Battle of Flodden in 1513.

The Battle of Flodden was a turning point for Scotland: The king was killed and the battle lost, leading to a gradual erosion of Scottish autonomy until the union of the crowns in 1603. The sixteenth century was also important to the towns because it was the century of the Protestant Reformation in Scotland. With the Reformation came the turning of the established church from Rome to its own authority, in a process that had long been a source of friction in the ecclesiastical structuring of the Scottish church.

The foundation of the burgh as a social form in Scotland—in light of this brief discussion of social and economic historical patterns—can be seen as one piece of a puzzle whose picture is one of national state making, with the town, the feudal estate, and the church all being important segments. Each of these entities represents certain cultural notions that were not new to the Middle Ages but were deeply engrained in European symbolic life. My interest in developing the three is in following the line of thought that leads to my main points about towns in general and about the ways that "town-ness" is expressed in civic ritual. Also in my cluster of theses laid forth in regard to the town, I maintain that the relation of the individual and the construction of the radical idea of individuality are connected to the formation of towns and to the structured social universe in which one can be at once a member of a corporate body and an individual citizen. Within the feudal system of inheritance by "blood" and rootedness in land and the church, of fixed-position selfhood, the individual person stands in a completely different relation to the corporation. I maintain that this is a crucial difference that is essentially tied to the modern and the Protestant in intricate ways.

The burgh is one frame for royal authority, giving citizens, or burgesses, the right to govern their domain, answerable to the council of royal burghs but not to the surrounding landowners. The feudal system of hereditary landholding, capturing for the king the allegiance of the landed barons, is another such frame. The ecclesiastical consolidation of bishops into "sees" and the implanting of abbeys are other frames for the same royal outreach and control, as is the creation of a court system in which the sheriff is answerable only to the king. The creation of burghs by barons and abbeys feuing land was another means of town construction in which one finds an ongoing series of skirmishes for power among the conflicting and contrasting entities of family, church, and town in the late Middle Ages that runs in and through other aspects of Western European culture in all its times and places.

Three different symbolic worlds exist side by side in these three set patterns of meaning and loyalty: In the inherited tenancies of lairds and barons the villagers and farm workers owed allegiance to the laird; in the church the monks and priests owed loyalty to the church; in the burgh the townspeople owed loyalty to the burgh; and the three different modes of thinking, believing, and owning land and collecting money were separate. All three eventually owed ultimate allegiance to the Crown and God, but the location of primary loyalties and the arrangement of cognitive landscapes within them were very different.

Here is my idea on "the town" in summary: The emergence of town as an entity—the creation of a civic space and a civic identity, including the notion of the public good and the concept of the citizen—is, in fact, tied up in a crucial way with the emergence of the notion of the "individual," that is, a person who can *leave*. The town as an entity is an incorporation, a body. The corporation of the *burgh*—the burgesses together as the citizens—is different from the *village*—an ongoing cohesive group of kin and coworkers but one that does not act as a body. The *town* as a thing or body is a cultural idea related to the idea of nation—or empire, hierarchy, kingship, the emergence of mercantilism and commerce—so that the medieval burgh created by the king was a new idea for Scotland in the twelfth century.

The burgesses were the merchants, the only persons recognized as individuals with the power to vote, decide, bargain, set prices, haggle, collect tolls, and ask for and arrange fair days—a handful of commercial men. Later on (as late as the nineteenth century) the right to vote for all property owners was granted, and then for all men. Finally, in the early twentieth century, this right was granted to women as well, so that every adult citizen was given the vote.

My thought is that the notion of "the individual" could not emerge in the social unit and symbolic world of village Europe or village Scotland, the laird–peasant worker arrangement. Nor, I think, could it easily be constructed within the village-to-city population that became the urban proletariat. Rather, it had to be created in a time and space and meaning framework of the town—the person as citizen.

What about the church in this cultural matrix? In the branch of Christianity that flourished in northern Europe and Scotland—that of the Reformed tradition—the notion of the individual is further drawn out in the understanding of being a citizen of "the kingdom of God." In this kingdom, God is the mayor, and the city is the city of God as lived in the corporate body of individuals that form a Protestant congregation. In the Church of Scotland and its daughter denomination of Presbyterianism in Ulster and America, the unifying notion of the Christian community is that of a covenant people, the direct recipients of a charter handed down by God, an establishment of the church as the chosen people, and the priesthood of believers and communion of the saints, all concepts thematically related to being citizens of a royal burgh answerable to the king. In the Protestant covenant community, God is the king, and the elect are the citizens of his kingdom, but it is *not* a feudal domain. Instead, it is a connected set of individual persons saved by Grace alone and not by their own good works. And they are persons who fit into or out of the towns of their origin in order to embark on an individual life as quest. In contrast with the mother church of medieval and Roman Catholic worlds, in which the person is rooted in a parish and answerable to a priest in ensuring his or her salvation, and in contrast with a village, where one is rooted in land, place, and "blood," the mother town provides a set of highly mobile categories in which persons can rearrange and become rerooted in other places as they follow the imperative of individual achievement.

The Making of "Town-ness" in Ritual

My contention is that the town is a master symbol—or a key cultural construct—in the array of constructs prefiguring the modern meaning of the individual and the corporate, that the mother is a key symbol in the construction of the meaning of the town, and that the common riding is the primary visible expression of this extended metaphor. This is the main thesis of this book, expressed here as really a kind of cluster of theses. In order to consider as valid (or even to begin to consider) my argument that these cultural realities are, in fact, possible and that they can be useful in understanding and analyzing the world of symbols, one must recognize that the larger imaginative forms of the town and its aesthetic self-fashioning are made up of a number of separate symbols of civicness, corporate life, and social segmentation within wholeness. The ceremony of the common riding itself can be seen as an elaborate processual metaphor for the town and the town's interpretation of its experience. The expressions of town, or corporation, of social divisions within the unity, and of boundaries and enclosed space all figure into the common riding imagery, along with symbols and meanings attendant to the ludic, humorous, and festive commentaries of feast and fair. Each of these deserves a more extended discussion.

Symbols of the Corporate and the Corporation

Ceremonial symbols representative of the civic and also the nation—in fact, of the unity of allegiance by individuals to a corporate group of many kinds—include uniforms, flags, emblems, seals, "chains of office," robes, sashes, medals, and crowns or caps. There are also, of course, the mace, cross, or banner to be carried high before marching lines of people; the sacred (or national) book, scroll, charter, or other writings often kept in a safe, secluded spot and brought out for ceremonies; and, often, holy places. In the case of the church, the holy places are the temple, shrine, or cathedral; and in the case of the town, the houses of local governance and courts, the market cross or the public square and other spaces sacralized by public ceremony, as in the parade grounds or, in the case of festivals, the streets. In addition to these material symbols and sacred uses of space to create sacred civic places, corporate power and personal obedience to it are often displayed in processions, parades, and other prescribed liturgies made up of dramatic and visual images and representations.

The best-known example of religious liturgy in the Christian symbolic world is certainly the Roman Catholic Mass, within which all the essentials of procession, banners, costumes, and sacred iconography merge with symbolically powerful gestures, such as bowing or genuflecting; kneeling; blessing water, wine, and bread; and giving and receiving these as having mystical power. In the elaborate liturgy of the Mass one finds merged all the right ingredients for galvanizing individual loyalties into group identity. The same is true for military liturgies—the military full-dress parade or review, for instance, or the elaboration of this into entertainment in Scotland known as "tatoo," and the highly ceremonialized military displays at official funerals, installations into high office, and other ceremonies honoring important national personages. In Selkirk all these sacred-to-civic and military images and symbols appear at the common riding and are played out in the elaborate civil liturgy on the town streets and at the boundaries of its common lands.[2]

Symbols of the "Social": Divisions Within the Whole

Although flags and banners are often seen as images of wholeness, as in required allegiance to the national flag and penalties for its desecration, flags can be successfully utilized as signifiers of internal segments of the whole, each requiring its own form of unconditional allegiance by members of the corporation within the corporation. This is true, for instance, of regiments in the army or of orders in the Roman Catholic church. It is also true of the guilds or "brotherhoods" in a traditional European social organization, the type of order associated with the medieval town. The guilds or craft brotherhoods call out emblems or images similar to those used by the church, the town, and the nation, in their symbolization of their unity and their corporate life over the individual members. Again, we find robes and uniforms, secret seals, handshakes, rituals, and mysteries known only to the "masters" of the craft.

In Scotland and the United States, especially in the nineteenth century, symbols and secrets of the traditional guild associations turned up on the modern scene as lodges and fraternities. The Freemasons, or the Masonic order, were the best known, but these also included in elaborate development in the United States the Order of the Elks, the International Order of Oddfellows, the Woodmen of the World, and, merging with the religious and crusading symbolism, the Knights of Columbus and the Knights Templar, as well as numerous other secret societies and fraternal organizations. In every state university in the United States, young men's secret societies calling on these kinds of symbols, knowledge, and rituals have also sprung up and proliferated since the late nineteenth century. Known simply as "fraternities," these brotherhoods are also heavily ritualized and use military, religious, and civic images often emphasizing those from the Crusades and knighthood.[3] The segmentation of the town into brotherhoods and their ceremonial appearance behind their flags in the foot procession and at the flag casting are important elements in the construction of Selkirk's common riding and its daily life throughout the year.

Symbols of Feast and Fair in Boundary Marking

Ceremonial observances throughout the Western world include the elements of celebration, feasting, and frivolity. Food operates here as a powerful unifier and also as a separator, for whoever eats together can claim membership, as in a family, an organization, a church, or other group of self-definition and exclusiveness. In the Roman Catholic Mass those who eat the body and blood of Christ are members of the Body of Christ in the church. An outsider is disallowed from taking part. In the Protestant outdoor tradition of family reunions and homecomings, those who eat together are a part of the "family of faith" and the "priesthood of believers," as I have argued elsewhere (see Neville 1987a). I view the outdoor meal of codescendants and cobelievers as a communion holding the same structural position as the indoor Eucharist but, in fact, expressing a symbolic inversion of the Mass into an antihierarchical form appropriate to enacting the unity of the "communion of the saints" in the Protestant sense.

The important days on the traditional calendar of the Roman Catholic church are known as both "feast days" and "holy days." Feasts and festivals accompanied the celebration of each patron saint of each town or village in medieval Europe and continue to do so in much of the Catholic world. Feasting is traditionally associated as well with celebrations of royalty or of military leaders at national anniversaries or war victories. As for the general public, the traditional feast day was one in which persons indulged in special foods with one's own family, kin, or friends. The indulgence in strong drink is an additional marker of group membership, festivity, and celebrations in general.

Food is not the only signifier of the festival and the fair; these occasions are also marked by music, dancing, games, contests, and general merriment. The kinds of events that fit into Turner's "liminal" phase of the rhythms of ongoing social life include masques, masquerades, reversals, inversions, and overall playing with the symbols of order and daily activities (see Babcock 1978, Manning 1973, Turner 1969). More than one scholar has suggested that in functional terms these periodic rites and rituals serve to continue the status quo by offering a kind of social and cultural "escape valve."

In symbolic and performance analysis the same idea is represented as the presence of irony, parody, satire, and comedy.[4] Games and contests provide the opportunity to display individual strength and skill within highly ordered sequences of sanctioned conflict or combat, calling on the repertory of symbols cherished by the culture. Those selected may also have special ceremonial value. Whereas, for example, the main sports enjoyed on a routine basis by Borderers are rugby, cricket, and football (soccer), the games at festive times most often include other sports. Horse racing is, for instance, held in Selkirk on only one day a year at a racecourse not used at other times, known as "the Gala Rig." Among the events of the festive weekend one also finds foot racing, gymkhana (horse- or pony-riding events of skill and luck), and Scottish dancing, a highly specialized and practiced skill.

The music for the common riding also is special, and there is a great deal of it. Songs of the Borders that are old and known to have been passed along for many generations join with songs that were composed by various Selkirk residents, exiles, and bandmasters. Many common riding songs were composed by one man who was the bandmaster in Selkirk—Christopher Reekie—in the late nineteenth century. Many of them have lyrics that speak of the beauty of the Borderland, the longing of the exiles for home and family, and the reasons that Selkirk is the brightest and best of all the Border towns. Songs and musical scores evoking a collective memory also are a powerful symbol of unity and comembership in the town, and the images they employ are those through which the town has constructed its own picture of itself and its present and past. Hills, sunshine (although the Borders are often shrouded in mist), roses in bloom, various pastoral scenes, dreams of romantic encounters, and memories of childhood are the images most prominently reappearing in the common riding songs. Every Border town has several bands, and Selkirk is no exception. There is, of course, the "silver band" that marches on Common Riding morning and plays the following day at the "games"; the "flute band" that is called in some towns the "fife band," whose main responsibility is to march around the streets of the town at 4:00 A.M. to awaken the people for the big day; and finally the "pipe band," composed entirely of bagpipers (primarily a Highland symbol, but one that has gained prominence all over Scotland for public display and performance.) All the members and leaders of all the musical companies are local residents; their band is their internal group of membership and identity in the collage of symbolic memberships that coordinate ceremonially to express the symbolic wholeness of the corporation of Selkirk.

The Town as Symbol
Warner speaks of town ceremony in Yankee City as "driving a deep shaft into the collective memory."[5] This is not to imply that all of the people in Yankee City actually remember the town's past but to assert that the town as an entity embodies a set of systematic symbols, rules, and meanings—one might call this the "culture of the town"—which, when called forth through ritual, form a significant statement about the town itself as it sees itself, as it conceptualizes its past, present, and future.

Towns, of course, are locations—collections of persons, not "persons" themselves. They do not "remember" or "symbolize" in the conventional use of these words, nor, of course, do cultures as entities do these things. Yet one imagines a town as being real, as having a "personality" or an ethos, experienced in the life of its people, visually stated in patterned spaces—streets and roads, a marketplace, a courthouse or city hall, a war memorial, monuments to heroes, a cemetery memorializing its dead, and buildings for commerce, worship, education, and residence. All of these features express the collective ideas of present and past generations and their notions of beauty and utility. The culture of a town's founders and its more recent arrivals delineate the town's composite lifeways, values, and ideas. The time period in which the town was founded and reached its prime and its past patterns of industry or trade shed light on the fashions and economies of space planning and architecture. This history of settlement, emigration, and the ups and downs of agriculture, commerce, and manufacturing should, then, be useful in understanding the town's concious celebration of itself in annual festival and civic ceremonial life. The arrangment of people into roles and groups as town citizens, council members, and planners of ceremonies is, of course, the key to how festivals are planned and to who decides what symbols to invoke. The relation of these social positions and their articulation within the fabric of town life are crucial to the outcome.

Town festivals and civic celebrations, like other cultural constructions, are not invented anew in each annual cycle or each generation but are made up of the available symbols known to the living as learned from the past. The persons of the present generation hold roles that are part of the cultural prescription for orderly life—such as that of citizen, town councillor, provost, or mayor—and thus have the deciding power to make the town ceremony happen. And yet the ceremony does not take place randomly or wantonly, and its elements are not created out of a cultural vacuum. Only the newest new town must make up its rituals, using the symbols and structures of past places and past meanings brought by the residents who have come with set ideas of what makes a town. In the established town, the established town festival has evolved over many years of celebration, adding an ingredient here, taking one away there, but always using as raw material the symbolic inventory of that town's culture and life.

In Summary, Selkirk the Town

Town ceremonies and town festivals are to town experience what poems, stories, plays and operas are to individual and group experience: These dramatic and poetic forms enlarge and enhance the daily routine, point to the crises, attempt to resolve contradictions, mourn the dead and offer comfort, and in general comment on and attempt to make meaningful sense of daily human life.

The *town* is, of course, only one form of settlement found in the cultural repertory of northern Europeans and their American descendants. There is also the *scattered open-country neighborhood* so typical of Celtic and Anglo-Saxon peoples (around what is known to culture-area analysts as the "Atlantic fringe") and so typical of the vast open country frontier of America, Canada, and Australia. There is the hamlet, or village, of the Anglo-Saxons, known to feudal system throughout Europe and tied to the countryside and the "county," itself an ancient administrative unit with an accompanying social reality as a set of interconnected lives over time that share a sense of place and loyalty.[6]

Later in the history of northern Europe and Britain, there is the *city* as a settlement form. Towns are distinctively Roman in their British version, having been introduced gradually from the South as centers of trade and craft specialization and as centers of power representing some distant empire of economic interest. Cities, too, came to Britain from the Continent and, along with cities and towns, the cathedral compound and the abbey and also the palace and castle, settlements symbolizing the rise of monarchies and the nation-state. The cult of *civitas*, the civic pride and awareness regularized in town organization, could be found in Greek and Roman towns and in their colonial implantations in very ancient times.[7]

The town today in Scotland and across the North of Europe shares with these antecedents numerous elements of cultural construction. But the Scottish burgh is also a distinctive creation of the distinctive history of Scotland itself, just like the establishment and persistence in Scotland of the open-country neighborhood, village, and city. Each of these forms of settlement—each community *form*—has its own specific ritual statements, including county fairs, village fetes, and elaborate tourist-oriented urban galas. Scattered communities of culture bearers living in isolation also have their ritual symbolization of meanings in the reunions of mobile people in the southeastern United States, Canada, and elsewhere in the "colonies." But for the town—in Scotland as, I venture to guess, for the town in northern Europe and America—the ritual statement, the performance of the place and the populus, is the town festival. In the Borders this is the common riding.

III

THE
INTERPRETATIONS

5

Anthropological Readings: Ritual, Symbol, and Experience

Anthropologists addressing the problems of performance analysis, the analysis of ritual, play studies, and the literary criticism of cultural texts sometimes work out their own puzzles as if the pictures they are assembling have separate meanings and can be discussed in entirely separate segmented "schools" of puzzle solving in separate languages of conversation. In my own attempts to understand and describe analytically the intricacies of the common riding, I have often been led down one or another path toward these separate outcomes as if they are mutually exclusive or, in any case, mutually unintelligible. Yet time and again I am drawn back to the central feature of the event itself as a series of actions embedded in its own particular historical and social setting with its own separateness and integrity, fitting into an overall pattern of meanings and symbols over time and space. There is a real event here. There are real horses and riders, band members and flutes, walkers in processions, and so on. And these people and their celebration are not easily fitted into anthropologists' categories, not easily explained by one or another pure and elegant theoretical system.

I have come to see the common riding as a number of things: as a *performance*, a kind of literary text expressing certain different themes and variations on themes; as a *ritual* enacting significant social processes; and as an event of festival and *play*.

As a text and a performance, the common riding is a romantic drama fitting into the tradition of Romantic poetry and fiction so familiar to the Scottish Borders. As such it uses the pastoral imagery of the familiar, of "home," and the pastoral forms of disguised royalty and inverted social position to make certain statements about oppositions between town and countryside, workers and nobles, townsfolk and "others." As a performance it calls on themes of heroic death in order to dramatize the town experience with losses through war and emigration. It also utilizes the symbolic inventory associated with Catholicism in order to restate traditional meanings that have been transformed from the mother church into the mother town. As Protestantism and capitalism have become implanted over time, a modernized Borders has at its heart a continuing traditional cultural center that, in the words of one local expert, "rears its head once a year on Common Riding Day."[1]

At the same time the common riding is evidence of a powerful ritual, providing a social statement and a social process, marking boundaries against the outside world, delineating internal groups and boundaries, and assigning a social position to the local citizenry that as a town have sent out their sons and daughters to wars and colonies and that have themselves remained at home to keep the town safe for tradition.

In addition to being a performance and a ritual, the common riding is also an event of festival and play. As play, the common riding is a set of elaborate behavioral patterns involving feasting, celebrating, drinking, dressing up, and generally enjoying life. All three of these aspects are eventually complex and culturally interesting. And all three refer to the lived experience of Selkirk's people and provide meanings for interpreting experience.[2]

Ritual, using multiple symbols with multiple referents in this instance, combines with performance and play in the elaborate staging and enacting of a collective representation that contains both commentative and transformative aspects. Both Weber and Durkheim could happily explain and analyze the common riding along with Kenneth Burke and all the followers of the traditions that these three giants represent. All the performance people could come with those who study ritual and symbolic expression, and the students of play could be there, as well as a whole wagon load of folklorists and ethnomusicologists, and there would still be enough going on for everyone—and each of their analyses would be in a sense "true" because of the immense complexity involved.[3]

In this chapter I summarize some of the material given previously, so that my readers might come with me along these analytical paths with multiple routings. The following are some of the main points I wish to have emphasized at the end of these parallel strolls down the paths of thought leading to the connections of symbol, ritual, and experience.

1. The common riding is a ritual that serves as a repetitive representation of the meaning of town. In its aspect as a ritual process, the common riding both reinforces the traditional Selkirk and places value on the older way of life associated with a world that is past. At the same time, the common riding transforms the modern Selkirk into a livable, doable, social form that can be handled within the local meaning system and value structure. It validates both leaving home and staying at home, thus constructing a cultural world in which the corporate—the town—becomes the mother of the individual. The seemingly opposing constraints of ongoing tradition and encroaching modernization are made temporarily compatible as they fit side by side into the ritualization of today's contradictions.

2. As a literary event—a performance—the common riding embodies themes and includes statements congruent with those in the Romantic movement of English literature, represented strongly in the Scottish Borders. It can be seen, in other words, as a romance. It creates the role of the person as self, as individual, and as citizen against the fixed position of the feudal manor. It idealizes the world of pastoral goodness extended to the town against the evils of the world beyond the boundaries, the unknown world of the outside, and the world of creeping industrialism in the mills and factories associated with modernization. It affirms the world of the real and idealized past against the world of the future with its unknown pitfalls and potential traps.

3. The symbols invoked in common riding imagery have powerful Catholic histories and histories of meaning within an older, more hierarchical, and more stable imagined world. As such, the symbols of town as mother and the accompanying symbolic paraphenalia representing town-ness and children of the town all work to find loyalties and ties that construct *corporateness* with the possibility of the *detachable individual*. We find here an example of the symbolic construction of a world that is congruent with the multivocal symbolic world of Protestantism and capitalism—a town that is mother, whom

one can leave in order to seek one's fortune and to which one can return—yet a world made up of transformed symbols from an earlier world of Catholic icons and emblems.

Finally, the idea of the individual person as a pilgrim going outward and of the life journey as pilgrimage fits here with the idea of pilgrimage in Protestantism. It is a construct within which individuals view their lives as pilgrimage and in which their return home is the inversion of the Roman Catholic pilgrim journey outward to shrines and places of miracles. In this aspect, the town ceremony (*civic liturgy*) fits with kin-religous gatherings (*folk liturgy*) as Protestant readings of Protestant experience, in contrast with the formal liturgy of the Mass in Roman Catholicism.

Holding together all these elements within the Common Riding drama are the repeated dramatic tensions (so fascinating to structural analysts) between the hierarchical and the communal forms of social order, between the open and the closed of modern and traditional systems, and, centrally, between the idea of the individual and the idea of the group. These are among the central conflicts that have driven the plots of great Western literature. The hero against the society; the hero affirming the "good," the conflict of hero with parents and with social constraints; the pull of traditional obligations versus the individual impulses for personal gain and personal glory; the tension of the idealized countryside against the stereotypical evil city; the town against the outside; and the idea of community against the idea of personal fulfillment—all these are variations on themes of tension in the construction of the town and the individual, crucial themes in the making of the modern capitalist world. The common riding is one story about the making of this world and its structures of meaning. It is a story about the sons and daughters of the modern world and about the Mother Town.

Common Riding: A Metaphor

This study has focused on one town among a set of towns in the region of the Borders of Scotland—the "Border burghs"—and on the distinctive civic ritual known as the common riding. In this sense, the ethnographic explanation concentrates on one culture, specific and ideographic, a microlevel of analysis within the possibilities of nomothetic theory and macrosociology. In another sense, however, the analysis and interpretation offered here can also be used generally as a key to unlock some of the secret doors of ritual and of culture and especially as a key to the door that leads into the large room of Western European culture and experience. The common riding of Selkirk is played out on a stage of moor and heath each year by players whose roles in everyday life are those of merchants, artisans, and workers, whose knowledge of the script comes from years of recurrent participation, each year the rehearsal as well as the performance.

The common riding is also an example of a larger script telling the meanings of towns through the European past, played out on a larger stage of history. It is representative in this sense of the readings that people in Western society have given of their own experience—of movement, nucleation, specialization of crafts, migration, tradition, and change. It contains elements of romance, tragedy, and comedy, its heroes found across Britain and the Continent in other versions in other stories, ceremonies, festivals, and celebrations. Its metaphors make statements that ring true for other Western townsfolk and their relatives in North America, Canada, New Zealand, Australia, and wherever Britons and Scots have gone to colonial destinations. The attention I have given to this one ceremony in this one Scottish town is not, therefore, merely a study of an exotic and colorful pageant to be filed away as yet another anthropological souvenir. It is—as the book title indicates—a study of the meaning of the town itself, of the town as a central figure in the social organization of Europe since Greek and Roman times and a key configuration in the shaping by Europeans of the colonial world.

An overarching processual metaphor is being enacted in the civic pageantry of the common riding. It is that of the town as mother sending out her sons to war and death, to the colonies, and to a "new life" that is beyond the death of leaving. She is a mother of guilds, trades, town common lands as property, and a mother of tradition, a representation of home for the mobile, wandering pilgrim who has followed the Protestant imperative to "leave home to seek one's fortune." What I have explored here is the notion that this entangled imagery of civic presence is in fact a Protestant reading of Protestant, modern, colonial experience and that it is one form of transformation, or inversion, of the world of Roman Catholic hierarchical forms. In the idea of the civic, the medieval bounded spaces and closed positions are found as a *corporate town*, and the modern unbounded open spaces of the individual person are found in the idea of the *individual citizen*—the colonial, the soldier, the pilgrim who is free to leave and return. The stayers and the leavers exist in a collage of meanings to give form to the entity we know as the *town*, the entity that has given form to both possibilities.

In other words, one message of this work is that the sacred world of mysteries and the Mass with its emphasis on death, martyrs, saints, miracles, and souls in purgatory can be seen in symbolic inversion in the secular world of rational individuals traveling outward to seek capitalistic, technical goals. The ritual structural expression of the first is, classically, the medieval church, and its liminal or antistructural phase is the Catholic pilgrimage. The Protestant structure is the loosely "unstructured" pilgrimlike journey of individual lives in counterpoint to its liminal phase of *return*, or reunion.

Between these two inverted worlds is a third universe of order—that of the civic universe, or town—not secular because it is sacred as home and mother (it is corporate as the body of the town), and not sacred because it is secular as the notion of individual citizen, the person who is part of the corporate group but free to leave and to travel outward as an individual. The civic entity is both church and the collection of individual members; one "belongs to Selkirk" as one "belongs to the church." The town is mother as the church is mother, and so the town is the church of the civic world. In this world the dead heroes are those who died in wars (just as the saints are "the dead who died in the Lord"), and the living heroes are those who have returned from battle with the hostile forces of the "outside world." Death is not only personal death but also collective death, as in the massive losses of the KOSB and the massive death of population through emigration (the emigrants who, not accidentally, became the heroes as ancestors in the American reunions).

I believe that the image of the town as played out in social form has had as powerful a metaphorical impact on our civilization as has the image of the church and the image of the individual and that the town and its ritual stand somewhere between these two key constructs in a conceptual continuum through which our notions of corporate group and isolated person have been created and passed on through generations.

Common Riding: A Ritual

One of the central theoretical problems of sociological theory is explaining the profound transformation in the nature of societies with the encroachment of modernization. A related problem is offering some clue to the processes driving this radical upending of structure, organization, and meaning. These concerns occupied most of the discipline's founders throughout the nineteenth century. In social anthropology a twin theoretical concern is explaining the relationship between social form and cultural expression accompanying these transformations in basic societal arrangements. Because social anthropology began as a kind of "comparative sociology," researchers in this field of social analysis have, until recently, focused on traditional, primarily nonindustrial and non-Western societies. Their data speak readily to the search for answers on this side of the question. Meanwhile, however, those whose interest has led them to look at the other side of the process continue the search for complementary data and answers—to research questions of continuity and change of symbolic and social forms in modernized, Western civilization itself.

One of the keys to unlocking the cultural puzzles of social change is, according to an increasing number of anthropologists identifying themselves as "symbolic anthropologists," the close analysis of ritual and symbolic expression. Here it is possible to study a "transistorized" version of a culture—a group's portrayal of itself in story, song, festival, ceremony, and performance. These tightly packed events, so the argument goes, are thought to "encode" information on culture in the way that microchips encode information in computer memory, or, at least, in ways that are roughly similar. In this book I have cast my lot with those who agree to use these rules, those whose belief and model of and for reality coincide with the understanding of culture as a symbolic code or set of codes that can be studied and in part deciphered through attention to images, representations, pattern, process and structure of action, and symbolic use of space and time, in other words, the study of ritual in its many and varied expressions. I consider also the changing social and economic meanings and arrangements that are going on at the same time, a kind of shifting and reshifting of order and meaning, a series of "skirmishes for meanings." I have focused on the symbols and scenes of a civic ceremony as a way of studying the processes of cultural statement and the cultural creation of reality within the overall context of a shifting and modernizing social and economic environment.

I am especially interested in the processes of the continuation of culture and the creation and recreation of "tradition" within the emigration of populations from Europe to North America and New Zealand. The ceremonies, gatherings, and other kinds of cultural performances among those who left their homes have served, among American Scots and Ulster Scots, as a means of ritually expressing some of the central features of Protestant culture and stating some of the underlying contradictions of the Protestant symbolic world. For those who remained behind in the towns of Scotland, other kinds of symbolic statements were made in song and story and, in the Borders, in the elaborate performances of civic ceremony known as common ridings.

These two ends of the thread of emigration—the reunions and homecomings of descendants of Scots and Ulster Scots in the southeastern United States (and also, I am told, in the Midwest, Canada, Australia, and New Zealand) and the town festivals in Scotland are connected through their place in the historical process of colonialism and industrialization. They are part of the overall pattern that sociologists call "modernization" or "secularization," the words used to describe a shift from traditional, medieval, and feudal worlds to modern rational–technical ones; the social transformation of gemeinschaft to gesellschaft that so interested the European writers of the late nineteenth century; and, crucially, from Catholic hierarchical worlds to Protestant individualistic worlds in the cultural galaxies of northern Europe.

In earlier work I detailed some of the ways that I think the Protestant worldview and experience are expressed and enacted through the distinctively Protestant cultural form of the reunion complex. I treat this as a "cultural system" fitting all the criteria of a pilgrimage, in the sense that Roman Catholic pilgrimages are "systems" within those cultural configurations to which they are important and powerful. This Protestant version of pilgrimage, I claim, is symbolically and structurally an inversion of the pilgrimage in Roman Catholic culture. As ritual processes, both of these pilgrimages are liminal to their routine, structured worlds and make comments on them and the conflicting elements—essentially unresolvable contradictions— of each culture's imperatives. And I brashly claim (in what one of my colleagues calls "my outrageous thesis") that one world presents an inversion of the other.

The common riding as ritual provides a second locale for exploring the way that symbols create and continue culture and the relation of symbolic forms to actual social experience. It ties together in a different way the Scots and the Scottish descendants overseas. It expresses further the intricate patterns of cultural continuity among these scattered people. The common riding analyzed as ritual also extends the exploration of the operation of symbols and meanings in one culture as it is found persisting (or "constructed" over and over again) over hundreds of years in one spot and then extending into the colonial empire abroad. Finally, this analysis broadens further the delicate process of excavating layers of meaning in cultural performance, embodying here a larger set of themes and motifs, explicit material symbols, and also a symbolic use of space, time, and human groupings in a rich display of pageantry and processional having elements of performance, ritual, and play.

In the common riding the rich liturgical formality of the earlier Roman Catholic and medieval worlds is stated ceremonially against the stark modern industrial routines of Protestant Scottish daily life (a liminal phase of structure, again, to be sure). We see a hierarchy of office and ceremonial status—summer kings and queens, military hero figures, processionals marked by banners from medieval guilds, regimental lines of horses mounted by townsfolk outfitted in regalia typical of country gentry and of nobility. We see emblems of civic pride—the flag, mace, provost's robes, and chains of office. We see the patterns of perambulation of boundaries—the riding of the common lands and the crying of the burley at the gates of the old town walls, marking ownership in the style of the rogations of medieval monasteries. There are songs and stories to go with this visual feast— songs of the mother burgh and the town as home, stories of war and death and lost young heroes, stories of the exiles who went away not to war but to colonial adventures and, like many of the soldiers, never returned from their conquests. The pageantry and poignancy, the drama of the ancient church and medieval town, the rootedness in the locality all come together in the common riding to give full ritual expression to some of the same contradictory demands of Protestant modern culture as seen in the American reunion.

These are the cultural imperatives to be both an individual willing to leave home in order to "seek his fortune" and a loyal citizen of a local community, in this case the burgh, or town. One cannot fulfill both these requirements, and therefore the reunions as pilgrimage frame one form of cultural expression for those who *traveled*, and the burgh's common ridings frame images and meanings in the same way for those who *stayed behind*. In both groups we find strong Protestant northern European symbolic forms in counterpoint with the earlier and more Mediterranean forms of Roman Catholicism and the medieval church. An exploration of these two ways of weaving a meaningful world through symbols gives us new materials for understanding the overall process of meaning-weaving in general. And it sheds light on some of the overall processes of the transformation of societies through reformation, modernization, and colonization. Finally, these slim rays of understanding open new questions about maintaining and creating ancient and new traditions among two equally modernized versions of one people, those who left home and those who did not.

Common Riding: A Literary Form and a Cultural Performance

The Romantic movement in literature of the early nineteenth century constructed a pastoral idyll of a world in the country and the nonindustrial towns and villages that is repeated in the world constructed in common riding imagery. The Borders was one of the idealized rural locations spotlighted by these anti-industrial poets, including Sir Walter Scott, whose novels hallowed the lochs and valleys of the Tweed and Ettrick rivers in an aura of unspoiled beauty. Both Wordsworth and Coleridge traveled to the Borders, and Wordsworth and his sister Dorothy met with Scott in the Ettrick valley near Saint Mary's loch and then wrote of this beautiful scene. Meanwhile, Scott was playing a double role in the drama of early nineteenth-century literature and life: He was serving by appointment as the sheriff of Selkirkshire and, as such, as cohort to the duke of Buccleuch. There are numerous stories of "the shirra" siding with the duke and the landed gentry against the plain folk of the town and the workers in the earliest mills. According to local tradition, Scott is famous for his quip to the mill owners: "You keep them poor, and I'll keep them honest." Playing a contradictory role as lover of nature and champion of the "folk," Scott was also writing the romantic novels that made him the toast of the land. This double identity and his picture of the simple life as an idealized world that had been lost is compatible with the emerging role assigned by contemporary scholarship to romantic poetry and novels in affirming in covert ways the social hierarchical arrangements that benefited the landed families and the manorial system in general.

Three different writers approach Wordsworth's poem "Michael" from this questioning viewpoint: "What is the 'lost world' and how/why is Wordsworth portraying it as he does in his pastoral writings?" Raymond Williams, in *The Country and the City* (1973), demonstrates that the Romantic pastoral poets mentioned here fit into the pattern in which, during the last two hundred years, writers of every age have claimed to witness the dying out of the timeless values of rural life, the rural life they knew in their childhood. Williams delineates the creation of a dichotomy between "country" (coded as good, true, and real virtue) and "city" (standing for wicked, false, and questionable morality) in the literature of Romantic poets and authors. Williams's student Roger Sales carries this to a further conclusion in the instance of Wordsworth and "Michael": He accuses Wordsworth and, by implication, other Romantic writers, of supporting the practices of feudalism and exploitation by landlords in the process of transferring attention to the urban capitalists as villains.

> What is Wordsworth trying to peddle in "Michael"? It is substantially the same product as he was trying to sell to the freeholders of Westmorland in 1818, for he is primarily concerned to divorce real estate, or economics, from concepts of estate. He does this, as suggested, by ignoring or evading questions of economic agency. Farmer's wives do not go to market. Ploughs drive themselves and fields are mysteriously burdened with debts. Strangers snap up property and an alien commercial system casts dark shadows over the landscape. Such an image must be seen as propaganda for the local gentry and aristocracy, as it conveniently ignores even the possibility that they might have been Michael's real enemies. (Sales 1983: 57–58)

A third analyst, Lore Metzger, accepts both these earlier treatments and goes beyond them to explore the mechanics of representation in and through the construction of a "world center" in the manner of Mircea Eliade's *axis mundi* as Wordsworth paints out the locations in "Michael" and other pastoral writings of the idea of home, the virtues of a lost community of "independence, equality, justice, and tranquility" (Metzger 1986:148). Metzger calls on Victor Turner's framing of transformative ritual in her understanding of the process through which the Romantic poets created their alternative world, transforming the real world of day to day into a "timeless paradisal pleasance" (Metzger 1986:201). Referring to Keats's hero in "The Fall of Hyperion," Metzger notes, "By eating and drinking consecrated food and wine, he has participated in a kind of symbolic death and rebirth. He stands at the threshold of a new life" (1986:203). As in Turner's treatment of the liminal phase of rituals, in these kinds of symbolic events and experiences, heroes and ordinary people are in the Romantic poems and novels placed in a never-never land in which the routines of daily cognitive schemes and rules of economic order no longer apply but are suspended temporarily or even dissolved (Metzger 1986:203). The manipulation of words, images, and ideas has enabled the construction of an alternative and a transformative world that exist side by side with the world of capitalistic economies and the realities of feudal exploitations.

I cite these scholars from English literary criticism because I find that the common riding as a dramatic performance lends itself to analysis as an expression of Romantic literature. Within the entwined

meanings and images of common riding symbolism and in the workings out of its dramatic process, both the mill owners and the "encroaching aristocracy" are targeted as villains against the pristine
virtue and order of the ideally unspoiled town. The central charac-
ters use the same devices as do the Romantic pastoral plays in the
woods, in which common people could dress up as nobles and nobles
could masquerade as shepherds in a true inversion of the social order—
but only for a day or a "midsummer night" in fantasy worlds enacted
on stages of locally sanctified natural beauty. In this "civic pastoral"
one finds all the themes of anti-industrial sentiment staged and
enacted by those whose livelihood is made as mill workers and commercial industrial workers. Themes of antihierarchical and antiestablishment sentiment are enacted by those who are caught in webs
of relationship with the surrounding estates of the dukes and earls
and with the officials of Parliament represented by district and regional councils and the ecclesiastical establishment of the Church
of Scotland.

The common riding as theater and ritual seizes on all the images
associated with the aristocracy and the nobility and turns these on
their head, for instance, in the use of horses and mounted processions
(essentially an elite symbol from the military and from hunting ritual)
and in the appearance of the standard bearer in elite costume as a
"summer king," hero, knight, whereas otherwise he is a simple working boy. For one day a year, the most important person in the Borders
is not the duke of Buccleuch but instead the standard bearer of the
town and, alongside him at the beginning and end of the ceremonies,
the town's provost in his regalia. On the nights of their dinners and
bussin's and at the moment of flag casting, this is so for the standard
bearers of each of the guilds and for their deacon. At the Common
Riding Ball the tradespeople and workers of Selkirk are decked out in
finery and become the dancers and revelers of the Hunt Ball of gentry, and they participate in the marches and formalities of court pre-
sentations and royal entries. Through the magic of transformative
ritual, all the world is turned upside down for one day, and Selkirk is
in a timeless paradise.

What I have attempted to do in this telling of the story of the
common riding and the interpretive analysis of some of its constitu-
ent scenes and their symbolic construction might be termed a "poetics of performance." This perspective, in Bauman's words,

> focuses attention on those framed, heightened, public, and symboli-
> cally resonant events . . . such as rituals, festivals, fairs, ceremonies,

and spectacles. . . . The densely reflexive nature of such cultural performances makes them privileged foci for cultural analysis: they are
cultural forms about culture, social forms about society, in which the
cultural meanings and value of a group are embodied, acted out, and
laid open to examination and interpretation in symbolic form, both by
members of that group and by the ethnographer. (1986:132)

By adopting this approach I reject others, namely, the exclusively
functional approach to analyzing ritual as directly expressive of economies or social interactions. Ritual, of course, does perform these functions, as it also provides an antistructure for the ongoing structures
of day-to-day life in Turner's terms. The Turners' analysis of pilgrimage does, in fact, deal with the same kinds of symbolic concerns that
I have treated here (Turner and Turner 1978). The analysis of ritual
as cultural performance accepts Victor Turner's insights into the way
that symbolic processes are ordered and then adds to them the insights
of others into the way that these same processes create meaning and
how the meanings then play into one another in the construction of
cultural worlds.[1]

Civic Liturgy and Town Experience

The town in Western Europe is a collection of citizens into a corporate body, just as in the same historical tradition, the church is a
collection of (if Catholic) "souls" or (if Protestant) "members." In the
church, as in the town, the individuals are "members of one body"—
the "body politic," the *civitas*, or the "body of Christ," the *ecclesia*.
In each of these the individual units relate to the whole in ways that
have presented an intricate puzzle, a favorite of those scholars given
to solving or attempting to solve the riddles of Western culture and
cultures in their various configurations. The puzzle is variously
framed as the "problem of the relation of the individual to the group,"
the "relation of self to community," the "contradiction of freedom
versus responsibility," or "free will versus the covenant," based on
whether one is a social analyst, philosopher, or theologian.

In literature and social theory, the town and church often appear
as metaphors for the restriction and limitation of freedom, for pro-
priety and close-knit relationships—the gemeinschaft—pitted against
the attempt of human beings to break loose or find personal identity
in quests for separateness—the gesellschaft of the sociologist, with
its negative effects of *anomie, alienation,* and *disenchantment.* In
cultural analysis, especially in the corner of anthropology that con-

cerns itself with symbols, these two contrastive themes and contradictory prescriptions for behavior present themselves as images within
a set of metaphors for other, deeper meanings at the cultural heart.

These themes and their expression in ceremonial life and social
experience are visible in the Scottish town. The towns of the Scottish Borders provide an appropriate locale for this inquiry because of
their classical form as ancient burghs in the model of the medieval
burgh, patterned on the purposefully established towns of Greece and
Rome. This form of creator-specific settlement was the device used
by the empire builders of classical civilization to extend imperial
influence into the far-flung regions of the Mediterranean world and
the margins of that world in northern Europe, and in Scotland the form
was used by the Anglo-Norman kings of the twelfth century to estab-
lish royal influence in the margins of their domain.

In the Greek and Roman version of town formation, a group of
colonists led by an appointed or officially sanctioned founder or group
of founders was sponsored by the imperial realm to lay out and inhabit its outposts as a mechanism of its cultural presence and social
domination. In Roman towns founded through this "budding" process, boundaries were drawn by a plow digging a trench around the
outer edges of town territory, and the town's center was established
by laying down symbolic markers, eventually to be enhanced by the
burial in the town center of the founders themselves as local heroes.
In northern Europe the creation and expansion of empires—first of
Rome, later of the Continental powers—resulted in the implantation
of administrative towns dotting the northern European landscape. In
Scotland, the Anglo-Norman kings implanted towns, or "royal
burghs," to solidify their control of warring families and to extend
the idea of the nation into the hinterlands. The Scottish burghs, then,
fit into the sweep of town formation, brought to light by archaeologists and art historians. Here I have attempted to construct a picture
of a particular *cultural form*—that of the "town"—as it expresses
some long-standing and deeply entrenched ideas about the nation,
empire, expansion, sponsored migration, founders and heroes, and the
interface between individual citizens and corporate bodies.

My production of this picture accepts the idea of the Roman
Catholic church as fused with the idea of the town. These two cultural forms marched together hand in hand across the European symbolic world as feudalism and other Roman ideas took hold. Against
this background, I have focused on civic ceremony in the Scottish Borders as a symbolic representation of "town-ness."

In the act of perambulating the boundaries through the common

riding I have described, the burgh reinforces its real or symbolic possession of common lands and at the same time constructs its image
of itself as an entity separate from the surrounding countryside dominated by the estates of dukes and earls, especially the duke of
Buccleuch. The ceremonial demarcation of its boundaries constructs
the town as an island of civic presence and civil authority—a kind of
city-state—against the feudal authority of the duke of Buccleuch, who
owns land adjacent to all the Border towns and whose vast estate in
fact surrounds most of the thirteen towns with a sea of aristocratic
private holdings. In the ceremonial riding of boundaries known as the
common riding, the town as a body constructs its corporate self and
makes visible the otherwise invisible reality of the corporate body of
town.

The individual appears in the pageantry and performance of the
common riding as the lonely figure of standard bearer representing
the person riding out ahead of the procession carrying the emblem of
the town, the burgh flag. The individual appears again over and over
as the local hero who captured an English flag at the Battle of Flodden
in 1513 and as the representation of heroic death in the individual
names engraved on the war memorial at the center of the town. Each
veteran of the British army is asked to join the procession as a member of the British Legion. It is the individuals who have emigrated and
returned who form another guild known as the Colonial Society to
walk in the foot processional that leads the horses back into the town
after the ride is completed. These persons are the products of the
experience of the town with emigration at the end of the nineteenth
century, when the woolen textile mills that once brought prosperity
disappeared in the wake of world recession and tariffs, sending waves
of Borderers into the "colonies." As the towns lost population through
the movement outward of individuals to seek their fortunes in the
capitalist world, the towns began to stage more and more elaborate
common ridings and festivals as statements of town-ness and perma-
nency, of motherhood and home for the impermanence of movement
outward into the colonial world of the emigrating young townsfolk.

Mother Church/Mother Town

The following images found in the common riding symbolism of the
town of Selkirk illustrate my contention that the town is portrayed
as mother, sending out her sons and daughters into the wars and
colonial encounters of the modern world, from which many never
return.

First, there is the mother and child on the burgh flag. This image is, for the residents and common riding celebrants, a powerful symbol of the town. The woman on the flag is said to have been waiting at the side of the road for the return of the Selkirk men from the Battle of Flodden in 1513. She is said to have been nursing her child, who was alive, though she was dead. Life and death are merged here, women waiting for men to return from wars, towns caught between lost battles and renewed hope. All the young men of Selkirk are said to have been killed at Flodden except for the hero Fletcher, who returned to the town to throw down the captured flag and then himself fell down dead. The themes of death and life appear in the closing ceremony of the common riding, when the burgh flag is cast in a figure-eight motion by the standard bearer in sequence with flags of men's guilds and the British flag. The casting closes with the plaintive tune "Flowers of the Forest," referring to all the young men who died at Flodden and in all the wars fought by Selkirk men with the "outside world."

Second, the motherhood of the town is further represented in the presence of the mothers of the fallen soldiers at the war memorial service, which forms an important segment of the civic ritual of Selkirk, as it does in every Border town. The mothers of the men are given particular places of honor. The devastation of the Borders regiment in World War I is referred to as Selkirk's "second Flodden."

Third is the standard bearer as a representative of the son. In order to fulfill this role, the young man chosen by the town council must have been "born on the burgh soil," which for many years meant on the soil of the "auld toun" or the Selkirk within the medieval walls. Mothers wishing their expected babies, if sons, to be eligible for this honor remain in Selkirk to give birth at the cottage hospital rather than plan to have their babies at the regional facility in nearby Galashiels or the urban hospital in Edinburgh. Parents save for years to help their son become the standard bearer for the town and after serving in the role, the young man so honored, almost without exception, remains in the town to work alongside his father and other relatives instead of following the lure of outward movement, as so many of his contemporaries do.

Fourth, the imagery of the town as home is embodied in the Colonial Society, locally known as the "exiles." The person who has emigrated will, if asked from what town he or she comes, answer, "I belong to Selkirk." In the same construction of meaning that attends the answers "I belong to the church," "I belong to the Masonic lodge," or "I belong to the Roberts family," the town's residents both in place and out of place conceptualize themselves as "belonging" to a larger entity in which they were born, rather than having joined voluntarily, and to which they can return, just as one returns to one's natal home. The concept and labeling of England and Scotland as home in the literature of the colonial period fit into this construct but are far too complex to include here except as a brief aside. In other words, Britain, or Scotland in this case, becomes the mother country to those who are her sons and daughters scattered overseas. Selkirk instantiates this belongingness in local place: mother town.

The material and this analysis are, of course, intended to illuminate more than the intricacies of one town symbolizing and celebrating itself. No matter how compelling the elegant construction of the civic ritual of common riding and its attendant images, it alone does not justify the resources, time, and energy expended so far in its study.

The enlarged importance of the common riding symbolism is, in my view, related to the convergence of its metaphorical statements with one of the underlying root metaphors in Western European culture—the metaphor of motherhood for nation, church, and town. It is not accidental (from the angle of vision of the structural and processual analyst) that the image of mother is found at the heart of symbolic expression in these social forms: the mother church as the body of souls and the body of the elect, the mother country as the birthing agent for empire, and "home" for the exiles, the sons and daughters of the motherland. The mother town stands in the same relationship, both symbolically and historically, to its members—the body of the corporation, the burgh as mother, sending out her sons and daughters over the generations to populate the vast expanses of the capitalist world and calling them back for periods of homage, as in the scattered souls whom mother church calls home. It is not surprising that within this collage of metaphors of motherhood the images of the Virgin Mary and their variations become emblematic of these complex relationships of person to group, citizen to country, soul to the church. She appears now as a madonna weeping for her son, caring for her infant, or giving solace to the poor and the needy; now as a secular figure in images of Marianne and the goddess of liberty; now as a "woman and child" waiting by the side of the road for the exiles and the soldiers to return.

I have suggested that the image of mother for various corporate bodies in European thought and experience is one that fits appropriately with a worldview deeply rooted in the traditions of civic nationalism and its ecclesiastical versions. The Protestant world with its

body of the elect refers to the same corporateness that is found in
Catholic notions of the body of Christ and the mother church, but
within a distinctively Protestant set of experiences and cultural configurations. And both Protestant North European and Catholic Mediterranean worlds are themselves multiple and pluralistic in symbol
and experience. I have attempted to add yet one more example to the
collection of examples and to suggest one interpretation that may
assist us in our puzzle fitting regarding the relation of person to group
and symbol to history in the analysis of the cultures of Europe.

Religious Symbols and Secular Ritual

Looking over the entire process of the ceremony from beginning to
end, we find in the common riding a number of separate symbols that
are historically and thematically related to the Roman Catholic,
medieval church. One of the most powerful images is that of the processional itself, an element so important to the liturgy of the Mass
that it was disallowed by the Reformers and does not appear in the
worship forms of any church of Puritan or Presbyterian heritage. The
procession of riders winding over the hills and stopping at three boundary stones for ceremonial proclamations and refreshments is reminiscent of the "stations" of earlier church processionals where priests
or monks would give prayers and blessings. In addition to the procession of horses, the foot procession with its internal segments and
banners is a classic medieval church form.

The notion of the common riding as perambulation can be traced
to religious observance of rogations in the medieval church. On Rogations Day, monks and priests perambulated their lands as a way of
marking their ownership, a practice also used in feudal law. As a royal
burgh, Selkirk had the right to ownership of its common land, and
the burgesses had the right to collect rent from those who grazed their
animals there as well as to collect taxes and tolls from all who traded
within the burgh itself. The "encroaching aristocracy" was, in the
past, a real threat to the burgesses' control. Selkirk town history is
filled with accounts of lawsuits between the town and the lairds over
use of the town commons, and even today the town remains surrounded by the holdings of the duke of Buccleuch. Over the years most
of the town's lands have been sold to mills and developers, so that
today the remaining commons are primarily symbolic lands. Their
perambulation is a statement of the town's integrity and its corporateness.

Focusing more closely on the emblems of the processionals, the image on the burgh flag carried by the standard bearer is a madonna with an infant on her lap, seen here as an example of transformed Catholic symbolism. The insignia of the burgh carries the multiple meaning here of the town as a mother, of the town as a fragile woman weeping for her dead and lost sons, husbands, and brothers and of the town as the bride of the hero who goes out to battle the evil forces of thè world and never returns to her. In Selkirk's past its young men have been lost repeatedly to wars and emigration. Its young women have sent their sons away to battles and the colonies. The mother town becomes a powerful image for this poignant process.

In the emblems carried by the foot processionals, one again sees transformations of religious to civic symbolism. Each trade guild marches together in set order, each one led by its own standard bearer carrying the flag of the guild. The insignias hold guild seals and dates of incorporation; the guilds themselves stand for older, traditional Selkirk life in which the trade guilds were significant groups in the town's political and ceremonial life well into the nineteenth century. Today none of these crafts actually functions as a labor organization or a political group. Their existence is strictly ceremonial and is seen by the public only on Common Riding morning. During preparation for the common riding, however, each of the guilds meets regularly for months to plan and to make preparations for their annual dinner and for the "bussin" of the guild flags in the Victoria Hall.

In the bussing of the flags we find yet another Catholic symbolic form, fused here with military imagery. In a ceremonial gathering, a special guest ties a ribbon resembling a battle ribbon on the top of the flagstaff of the guild flag, adding to the ribbons from previous years; speeches are made to wish the guild standard bearer well; and the town songs are sung in chorus. This ceremony is as near to the "blessing of the flags" or the "blessing of the troops" as one could expect to find among Protestant people. Even closer to a ceremony of "blessing" is a ceremony known as the "kirkin' of the cornet," held on a Sunday morning before the day of the common riding in the parish church of some Border towns, although it is not held in Selkirk. In the parish church of Selkirk, the guilds and their flags had a special place for hundreds of years. The civic and religious symbols were entwined in such a way that each of the ancient guilds had a special spot to sit together under their banners in the parish church. This practice continued long past the Reformation.

In addition to the perambulation, the processional itself, the emblems, and the custom of the "blessing" as referents to traditional society, the music of the common riding also refers to an earlier medieval and Roman Catholic world in both their form and content. Many of the songs of the common riding come from the older forms of folk tunes and from carols. Carols and musical chants, so central to Roman Catholic liturgy, were banned from church use at the Reformation and remained in disuse in those regions where reformed Protestant worship took on its most austere expressions. Yet the carols and songs of the common riding are sung in the schools and in the pubs, and on Common Riding morning they are sung in the streets in a set order of performance as the silver band makes its rounds and then in a set order as the band leads the horses back in from their boundary ride.

The words of the opening song have an especially powerful symbolic referent. "Hail Smilin' Morn" celebrates the coming of dawn, the "smilin' morn that hails the break of day . . . in whose bright presence darkness flies away." These words repeat themes of light over darkness and the symbolism of good over evil that are strong in the image of the town as a center of light, truth, and civilization against the powers of the night. These powers include the powers of war and death and the generalized evil forces in the history and economy that are sometimes personified in song and story as individual dukes and earls who have threatened the town's autonomy.

The symbolism of death is pervasive in the common riding imagery, just as it is in the Roman Catholic symbolic world. The death of the young men of Selkirk at Flodden is mourned musically in the plaintive melody of "The Liltin'" after the last flag is cast in the market square. As "The Liltin'" wafts out over the silent crowd, it is the flag of the British legion, or the "Union Jack," that is bowed to the ground during the music in homage to these dead young men. The ex-soldiers hold a special memorial service at the town's war memorial at 5:30 A.M. on Common Riding Day, placing flowers on the monument and bowing in prayer to honor the dead of the two world wars. The death of those who leave the town for the colonial, capitalistic enterprise is also pervasive, another theme of untimely death, draining the town of its fairest and finest young men. The local Colonial Society consists of those who went away at some time but later returned to live in the town. Each year its ranks are swelled at common riding by returning "exiles," Selkirk folk who have emigrated but who return periodically for this holiday reunion with friends and families.

There is also the symbolism of home—here not a heavenly home but an earthly paradise. At the Colonial Society dinner the songs of the Borders and of Selkirk speak especially poignantly of the longing for a lost home. Returned exiles sing "Borderland, my Borderland, my first love and my last . . . Selkirk, oh Selkirk, she's ancient and she's braw. . . . Of all the bonny Border toons she's the fairest of them all."

The Colonial Society's celebration of return home enables the temporary resolution, through ritual, of the long-term unresolvable dilemma of Protestants and capitalists everywhere: One cannot at the same time *leave* home to seek one's individual fortune and *stay* home to become a pillar of the community. The industrialization of Selkirk in the middle nineteenth century placed its young men in a position of irreconcilable conflict. To leave for personal advancement was to become dead to one's town and family. But to stay was to gain local community position at the expense of individual advancement in the outside world. This dilemma remains before the young men of Selkirk, and it is resolved temporarily in the ritualization of the common riding. The "stayers" are honored as standard bearer, attendants, ex–standard bearers, and members of a ceremonial men's club based on the ancient guilds. The "leavers" are allowed to return with honor as members of the Colonial Society, to affirm the virtues of the town they chose to leave so many years ago.

The recurring story that enfolds the imagery of the common riding is the story of the Battle of Flodden. The defeat at Flodden is a metaphor for the defeat of Selkirk in all the wars over the years, most recently in World War I, in which hundreds of young men from the Borders were killed on one day at the Battle of Gallipoli. It is also a metaphor for the defeat of Selkirk in its battles with dukes and lairds who encroached on the common lands, with mill owners who transformed the town into an industrial center in the 1800s, and with Parliament which, through burgh reform acts, again and again has taken power from the burgesses and given it to those of the "outside world." Flodden also stands for a lost battle with emigration, which drained the town of its young men, dead to the town socially by leaving to seek their fortunes as individuals.

The town is depicted ceremonially as a fortress defending against the forces of "the outside world," just as the medieval church was seen as a fortress fighting the powers of darkness. The standard bearer becomes a symbol for belonging, courage, virtue, and heroism. He must have been born on the burgh soil; he rides out to protect it as its hero and returns the flag "unsullied and untarnished." He is crusader, knight, hero, defender of the faith, and guardian of the town honor. The league of ex–standard bearers who have successfully performed this defensive task march in close order double file on the night before the common riding and silently place a wreath on the statue of Fletcher, their ancestral hero-founder. The standard bearers have been born in the town and have remained there through their lives to become merchants and workers and to appear at the common riding in a place of honor.

I have enumerated certain specific symbols and also the over-arching symbol of Flodden. We ask now about just what we are seeing in the symbolic clothing of the common riding. The town is clearly being portrayed here through an elaborate tapestry of individual symbols as a greater, extended symbol itself. The key to answering the question of why Roman Catholic imagery would be used in these ways by Protestants in a Protestant country lies partly, I believe, in the understanding of Catholic and Protestant symbolic worlds in social and economic as well as religious terms.

Here is my guess at the answer: Even though the church in Selkirk became Protestant at the Reformation, the worldview of Selkirk remained essentially Catholic and medieval until the mid-nineteenth century, when a process was set in motion that I call "Protestantization." An examination of the burgh history reveals that the burgesses were in tight control of power and privilege over the centuries until the Burgh Reform Act of 1833. The town was virtually isolated from the outside until 1830 when the first road was built to Galashiels, a neighboring industrial textile town. By the time the first railway came in the 1860s, the burgh was already the location for the industrial manufacture of woolen textiles in water-run mills along the Ettrick River and then steam-powered looms, built with the new capital from Galashiels. Mill owners moved into the town and began to assert their power; mill workers moved in from the country and took their place as "workers" and "citizens." Beginning in 1830, the population doubled and tripled, until it reached its all-time high of almost six thousand in the 1880s. Protestantism as a worldview and as a way of economic life was finding its way to Selkirk.

Until this radical shift in political and economic organization, in which the view of the person shifted from a position in a fixed order to focus on his or her skill as an individual and a worker, there is no evidence that the Selkirk after the Reformation was very different from the Selkirk before. The members of the parish kirk attended services, listened to preaching, sat with their guilds, paid fees and tolls to the merchants, memorized the catechism in order to be confirmed, were admonished to repent their sins, were given various kinds of expiation—"works" before the Reformation, public ostracism or flogging afterward—and formed processionals in the streets on ceremo-

nial days. The parish remained coterminous with the burgh; the medieval walls formed the general boundaries of settlement; the guilds and
the burgesses held sway; and the population remained stable for about
eight hundred years. Industrial, Protestantized Selkirk was born out
of the textile mills. A whole new town had emerged in fifty years'
time, sprawling outward from the old.

The first Selkirk, the Catholic and medieval one, was created out
of royal decree and implanted as a burgh within a feudal domain. The
second Selkirk was a prosperous and thriving industrial mill town that
was the receiver town for thousands of country folk who had left their
villages to become workers in the mills. There was also a third Selkirk,
a sender instead of a receiver. Its young men and women answered
the challenge of the colonial empire when world economic forces
drove down woolen prices and caused the mills to close, beginning
in the 1890s. Townspeople who saw no future in Selkirk for personal
advancement left the town in the now truly Protestant spirit of individualism to seek their fortunes elsewhere, in the cities—Edinburgh,
Glasgow, London—or the British Empire—Canada, Australia, New
Zealand, Africa, India.

The Selkirk of today, fourth in the historical series, is a thor-
oughly modern, Protestant town in every way, with new firms having come in to take over old mill buildings and to build new facilities
for assembly plants of electronic equipment and printed circuit boards
for the computer industry. The incomers at this point are middle-class
middle management, people who drive cars and cross the boundaries
from town to town for work and residence, people who take part in
parent associations at school and run for election to the Ettrick and
Lauderdale District Council, which replaced the older burgh council
by parliamentary decree in 1975. Old Selkirk has now lost all its formal political town autonomy to the districts and regions, in the process that London styles as "regionalization," the final blow in the
British government's one hundred-year campaign to remove the
burghs from local control.

In the common riding, all four versions of Selkirk the town find
enactment and expression. In the common riding the symbols of the
feudal burgh of Roman Catholic Norman Scotland create a magical
transformation of the new rational–technical order. The incomers are
outside the symbolic world; the old walls become the boundaries again
for one day; the common lands belong to the burgesses once more;
the returning hero-knight goes out to conquer darkness and returns
victorious in a reversal of history as the burgh recreates its past;

colonials return for reunion dinners; and ex-soldiers come back from the wars. The Protestantization of the burgh is suspended temporarily in order for the traditional Catholic and medieval one to hold center stage.[4]

Summary: Ritual, Symbol, and Experience

In summary and in conclusion, what can be said about the symbols and meanings of the common riding that will inform us about the way that symbols work generally and about the processes of symbolization as part of larger historical and economic processes? The common riding, like an opera or any other work of art, whether painted, composed, sculpted, or performed, invites multiple interpretations. I suggest here four different aspects of this particular civic–religious ritual that may be generalized and explored in other contexts.

1. Individual symbols from a Roman Catholic symbolic inventory are summoned here to express meanings that have to do with civic and secular themes, with "town-ness," but with certain particular aspects of town-ness that call up values of tradition, order, and continuities of the real and created past. If we assume with Weber (1958) that the Roman Catholic symbolic world is one of traditional authority and order and that the Protestant worldview is an individualized, personal quest in a social environment that is increasingly rational-technical, legal, and mobile, then the common riding symbolism refers to a worldview that is essentially Roman Catholic or traditional. Protestants in this case call on Roman Catholic symbols to express particular meanings associated with particular traditional values, values associated with an older, safer world in which the order is unchanging.

2. Beyond the referents of the individual symbols, there is also a larger picture constructed by the total unfolding event. The common riding is a processual metaphor for the town itself, the town of the imagination. It is a town that has the shape and form of the medieval church. In this overarching processual metaphor, the burgh is the mother, nurturer, and intermediary between the people and God, the protector from the powers of darkness on the outside, just as the medieval church was all these to its people. The burgh is the mother of the processing horsemen and the standard bearer, just as the church was the mother of the monks and the priests. The burgh is the sustainer of life, the giver of privilege, power, and punishment, as was the ancient church. The separate guilds are not only civic but also religious "orders," just as they were in ancient times in the church-

ordered society; the returning soldiers and colonials take their place in the church repertory of roles as returning crusaders and pilgrims, heroes who venture out but always remain rooted in the established order of burgh–church life. The bounded town walls and town lands create an exclusive territory of corporateness, just as the church creates its own corporateness. The burgh corporation is the body of the town, of the *civitas*, just as the church is the body of the *ecclesia*.

In the metaphor of the common riding, the town-church is also itself a symbol of order, local authority, and the ongoing unchanged power structures of the past. The town as church is a safe haven from the seas of sin, an island surrounded by those who seek to encroach on its sanctity, a sanctity that must constantly be protected with symbols and rituals from those who would destroy its sacredness and integrity. The church-burgh is the essence of home in a world with an increasing sense of homelessness, a world that is becoming segmented, individualized, and nonhierarchical.

3. The symbolism of the common riding not only affirms the old values of tradition but also fuses the new world with the old in ways that make the new world bearable and intelligible. The alternation of leaving and returning represented by the British legion and the Colonial Society makes a ceremonial statement of what has in fact been true in history: Some townsfolk have left and have died a social death never to return, whereas others have left and have come back from the dead. And still other folk have remained behind in the town to work in the mills and new companies and be merchants, to carry on the tradition of the royal and ancient burgh while at the same time coming to terms with the changing modern British world.

Meanwhile, the burgh itself has undergone rhythms of economic life and death. It swings into prosperity or decline in response to swings of unfathomable trends and outside forces, yet it survives in repeatedly reconstructed hybrid forms. The burgh is not only the medieval church; it is also the Protestant version of this tight-knit collectivity. The civic entity of the "town" is a transformation of the Roman Catholic bounded and hierarchical social form of "church" into a partially bounded entity of stayers and leavers whose rhythms of dispersal and return mark the alternations of civic life and economic health.

Town ritual, then, expresses meanings of both the traditional and modern social orders. It must include both Catholic and Protestant elements in order to accommodate both sides of the town's experience and both sides of its world of meanings. This process of cultural construction and reconstruction through ritual is seen especially in archaic societies that are modernizing. It is a process through which changing societies have seized on symbolic expressions, reversals, inversions, recreation of history, ritual, ceremony, and performance in an attempt to resolve the contradictions inherent in the breakdown of the old order and to make the new order intelligible.

4. As an example of town ritual in Western society, the common riding stands somewhere between the two extremes of Catholic and Protestant ritual processes that I have described and discussed in my own recent work on rituals of reunion in American Protestant culture. My studies of the symbolic expression of Scottish descendants in the southern United States revealed a set of elaborate gatherings of kinfolk and cobelievers that I have identified as a pilgrimage complex among those who have left home to pursue the Protestant ideal of individualized fulfillment. I suggest that the rituals of reunion—which include family reunions, church homecomings, cemetery association days, camp meetings, and denominational conference summer communities—frame one end of a continuum of types in symbolic social form. It is a type that is outdoors, nonhierarchical, antiestablishmentarian, and open. I suggest that this type expresses an inversion of its antitype, the Roman Catholic Mass, which is indoors, hierarchical, established, and closed. I argue that each is the symbolic expression of a world, Catholic or Protestant, and that the second is an inversion of the first. I am now suggesting that the civic ceremony of the Scottish town is an example of a midway form of ritual statement in which both these two sides of Western Christianity find expression. Town ceremony is, in other words, at the same time outside in the streets and fields and inside the town walls and lands; it is unbounded yet bounded in its structure. It is nonhierarchical in its celebration of equal citizenry and the equality of all who are Selkirk folk born on the burgh soil, but it is hierarchical in its careful placing in rank order of the older traditional guilds and crafts and its own local royalty of standard bearer and attendants. It is antiestablishment in its statement of local authority and control against the power of dukes and earls, yet it is establishment in that it creates its own internal criteria of selective membership, power, and privilege. And although it is open on the surface to all who wish to march or sing, it is, in terms of real inner participation, essentially closed.

The Protestant symbolic world, with an emphasis on individualism and personal achievement, represents a transformation of the medieval, Roman Catholic world of structured, church-based burgh life. In the symbolic world of the Scottish town, these two worlds live side by side. The structured social order of older burgh power and privilege finds its place alongside that of the newer, loosely structured, mobile, modern universe of mills and microcomputer companies. The meanings of the new compete for prominence with the meanings of the old and exist, finally, side by side in an uneasy truce. The common riding affirms that the new order has been created out of an older one—that 800 years of tradition stand before the 150 years of creeping modernization—and that the new world is doable and bearable precisely because it was born from the old. Both find expression in the symbolic world of Mother Town.

Epilogue

We anthropologists working in highly textualized cultures, such as those of Western Europe, often find ourselves overwhelmed by the wealth of our ethnographic materials and by the inadequacy of our method in dealing with centuries of written texts. We face the further intimidation of answering critics who read our work outside their own elegant expertise in some aspect of cultural or social analysis— folklore, ethnomusicology, literary history and criticism, sociocultural and economic history—not to mention the contemporary experts who find their voices in fields of "Scottish studies," "British studies," or "European studies." To make matters even more complicated, those of us growing from ethnographic backgrounds have to answer the voices of our former teachers and mentors, calling from beyond retirement, or sometimes from beyond the grave: "Why have you forgotten the basic tenets of (say) community study, or ritual process or holistic description, or cultural ecology or structural- functionalism or sociolinguistics (or whatever particular school of thought happened to be our own brand name in anthropological enculturation)?" To these potential interpreters and anti-interpreters of our efforts are invariably added the voices of "our people," the true experts on their way of life or their civic ceremony, but even they themselves, as we well know, have varying readings of local texts, and so we face the somewhat ominous task of selecting those to which we will give attention. Herein lies a source of potential paralysis in producing a written text of one's own.

In this presentation I have, like the fox, pursued many things: the idea of home, the concept of person and group, the enabling structures of leaving and staying in the migration processes, the formation of identity in the face of depopulation, and the symbolization of stability, separation, and power. I have chased after the elusive problem of how ceremonies "work" and how they "mean" and the even more elusive problem of how we as ethnographers are to talk about workings and meanings and so bring them into being for our own conversations. I suggest that ceremony can be viewed as performance, ritual, and play, and then I go about performing an analysis with the ritual purpose of publishing a book. Some of my colleagues can catch glimpses of my own play of words and of ideas, for the process of creating this analysis out of the lived experience of fieldwork has been—mostly—a pleasure.

As an epilogue, I have chosen to reconstruct my own understanding of the three terms key to my unfolding narrative—symbol, ritual, and experience. Why, in other words, have I chosen as a subtitle these three words instead of others, and what are my own individual meanings of them as I inquire and write? What follows is essentially the definitions of these terms as I have come to understand and use them in this work.

Symbol

Symbols, in my understanding, are condensed locations of meaning in cultural arrangements of various "raw materials" of human group life. In the study of civic ritual presented here, these include *material paraphernalia* (icons, statues, costumes, ritual objects), *words* (speeches, talk about ritual and talk within it, descriptions of ritual and its meaning by participants, observers, and reporters) *music* (songs, tunes, instruments, and performative contexts), *dramatic staging* and enactments (processions, cavalcades, scenes at stages of a procession or cavalcade, scenes of handing over and returning flags and "bussin" flags as well as the official "blessing" of flags and their carriers), *use of space* (where people walk, sit, and stand and in what order; where ceremonies are held and not held; what kinds of spaces are used by whom) *sequencing of time* (use of early or late hours, reversal in usual daily time or calendar time, timing of performances and public events), *aesthetic forms* (architecture, town planning, statuary, church placement and exterior and interior design, public buildings, monuments), and, not insignificantly, the *economics of making a living* (meanings of work and vocation, status, class, and power expressed in ritual, meanings of money and other media of exchange, and the social and historical contexts within which these economies have developed and changed). This definition of symbols implies that everything in human culture is symbolic. This I would agree to as a beginning definition of culture itself—the sum total of human symbolic behavior or the human capacity to endow otherwise meaningless nature and social activity with symbolic order and significance.

According to this broad definition of symbol and culture, every aspect of human social conduct becomes communicative and expressive, even those accommodations to human need so cherished by functionalists—food, shelter, and reproduction. Food is highly culturally specific, and in one cultural location food becomes proper food for various occasions. What can be more heavily imbued with meanings than the notion of "shelter," including houses and their arrangement and decoration and also the expanded notion of shelter through social groupings and religious arrangements? Reproduction under human culture also takes on the elaborate complexities of kinship, family and household, descent, and so forth. These expanded definitions seem superlative if not simplistic to the cultural anthropologists who have learned through years of graduate study to take them for granted and to assume the symbolic properties of culture as the basis for humans to evolve and to live in diverse worlds. Yet for the benefit of the casual reader of anthropology and the not-so-casual scholar seeking to discover from us some sense about humanity, these meanings that we hold as part of the culture of anthropology must be made explicit from time to time.

Symbols are never limited to one meaning or set of meanings but are constantly in the process of constructing and reconstructing their meaning by the groups that have seized them as modes of expression. For instance, in one time period a particular symbol—such as the mother and child—may have different meanings for different groups within a town, depending on the people's social position, their siting vis à vis the powers of control, their past experience of history learning or story listening, and their record of participation in civic ritual. The same symbol also has different meanings over time for each of these groups and situations, so that it takes on a history of its own— a "life of its own," in cultural terms—and can be studied by itself as a kind of index of social and cultural change. Again, the multivocality and polysemy of symbols are not new to anthropologists, but they are so embedded in our worldview that we should be wary of using the concepts unexplained in writing for broader audiences.

Ritual

By ritual I mean the organization of symbolic behaviors and orders into set patterns of recurrent appropriate forms that have meaning for a particular people at a particular time. Like symbol, ritual is a concept packed with hidden understandings for various hearers of the word. For anthropologists it has taken on a kind of middle range meaning somewhere between functionalism—ritual "functions" to alleviate anxiety à la Malinowski or to create anxiety à la Radcliffe Brown—and performance analysis. Ritual is a drama that can be understood through a literary analysis of its inclusive tropes and their structure and meaning.

In the ritual process, moving through time and life cycles of symbolic enactments and performances, symbols are selected and discarded by the makers of culture. The symbols used are significant for their choice and their referents; likewise, the symbols not used are significant for their omission. In ritual the symbolic codes of a culture's rules and meanings can be called out and displayed. In ritual and through participation in it, the bearers of a culture have a way of experiencing, remembering, and telling a story that places their history on a larger stage of history. Ritual marks human life and collective life, and in this sense it is a context for symbolic expression in which life cycles and their interconnected patterns into human communities are assigned meanings within overarching cultural meanings that may be common to whole language communities or to entire "civilizations."

Like symbols, rituals have multiple meanings that are different for the various groups that use and celebrate them to create different meanings based on social, economic, and other cultural positionings. And like symbols, these meanings change over time.

Experience

Somehow for anthropology, experience is a more difficult term to capture in a definition than is either symbol or ritual, although these two are in themselves problems. By experience I mean the lives of people in real places—towns and countrysides in Scotland, for example, as in this particular ethnographic locale. These lives hold rich and complicated meanings in their unfolding patterns of work, play, marriage, giving birth, teaching the young, gaining status, going to war or to the colonies, or staying in the town to become one of its long-term citizens. And the experience as reported, as interpreted in story and song, and as verbalized in prayer and commemoration of the dead makes up the fabric of cultural experience of the town itself as a transgenerational series of lives. Experience is related to history and economy, which is why I have included both historical and economic narratives in the main story line of symbolic expression. It is from the persistence of cultural materials and interpretations over long periods of time that an important part of history is made, and the same is true of economics. Civic ritual—and all rituals that give visible expression to meanings—is constructed from the inventory of symbolic materials stored in a people's history and from the meanings they have assigned to goods, labor, and capital.

Again, my caveat comes: Experience, too, is culturally defined by time, place, and position. Any reading of a town's or a person's "experience" must be taken contextually for that town or person as well as contextually for the interviewer-interpreter. Within these very fragile proscriptions, the work of ethnography continues.

Power and Politics in the Making of Ritual

In these definitions of symbol, ritual, and experience, I have not emphasized their political dimensions and significance in the assignment and continuation of power. Who says what a symbol means, for instance, and which symbols are selected for what political aim? Which version of the ritual is to be performed, and who are to be the main players? Whose version of experience is to become the "official story," and in what ways does this articulate with the multiplicity of "unofficial stories" (usually called *folklore*, as opposed to *history*). These questions must, of course, be addressed. Their very omission from numerous symbolic analyses is in itself a political statement, as we are reminded frequently by critics of symbolic anthropology and by members of each of the groups whose versions of official stories have not been allowed to be told. The manipulation of symbols and the skirmishes over ownership of tradition remain issues central to the study of culture, and it has been my intention to write my text with the assumption that it is these intertextual conflicts and their resolution and reresolution that create one underlying scenario of symbolic social life. The interplay of meanings and the making of meaning with power and the uses of power remain an important arena in which the ethnography of expressive forms is being invented and reinvented in anthropology today.

In Summary

Finally, it has been my intention to tell the story of the common riding in such a way that the reader can reconstruct some of the order, structure, and symbolic expressions of the event and to know what actually happens on the streets and in the fields of Selkirk on the first Friday after the second Monday in June. With this in mind, I have alternated descriptions of people moving about on the landscape with my understanding of the meanings of these movements. I have described the participants and their social standings, occupations, ages, and costumes with the idea that the reader can infer with me some of the meanings of their positions in the ritual. And I have described the dramas of war and emigration along with the dramas of the coming of the mills and their later decline for the purpose of placing experience in touch with its enactment through symbols. My interpretation and analysis come side by side with my attempt to describe the events, for I am fully aware that no description can be purely "objective." The sources for my knowledge of the common riding—my observation and participation over time along with reports and stories from long-term Selkirk folk—are themselves a product of siting and situating. Yet I present them here as one representation of truth and truths, a representation of reality as seen by one ethnographer in the tradition of symbolic anthropology and interpretive method.

I present here the story of one town and one civic ritual as an example of other towns and other rituals, whose stories are different and yet have certain similarities. The towns of northern Europe and their colonial daughter towns around the world are examples of structures of corporateness within which individuals are citizens and as such are free to leave or stay. The civic rituals they hold as ceremonial enactments include numerous variations on themes of town-ness and the town as mother and home—national holidays such as Fourth of July, local versions of civic nationalism such as town anniversaries or town homecomings, "town festivals" created for self-fashioning and tourist entertainment, memorial days for the dead soldiers of particular wars or all wars, and in the Roman Catholic towns various celebrations of patron saints' days with civic and national undertones and overtones.

In these kinds of celebrations honoring the town and the nation, one finds the use of varieties of symbols common to European culture—flags and banners, processions and parades, horses in mounted cavalcades, chains of office and official robes or scrolls, "keys to the city" (in Scotland, "freedom of the burgh"), speeches by dignitaries, the laying of wreaths, and the military salute or march past. The civic rituals are embedded in a fabric of preparations by clubs, orders, brotherhoods, and societies of all kinds, including political and ostensibly nonpolitical associations. There are dinners, honorary awards, trophies, telegrams, building of stages and their dismantling afterward, placement of furniture, preparation of food, entertainment of visitors, and provision for the principal actors in the public parts of the event.

In my attempt to assemble some of the available texts and arrange them into a text of my own in some intelligible way for other readers and writers, I have selected for my focus the performed text of civic ceremony as a place to begin. In so selecting I have automatically eliminated numerous other rich sources and materials, and I have automatically limited my analysis to certain segments of the town's life and work at the expense of others. For instance, I do not treat in any detail the daily routines of the merchants and tradespeople or even the local workings of agriculture, commerce, manufacturing, or banking; I omit sports, which are important to the Borderers, and club life; I mention only in passing the growing number of professional and bureaucratic residents; and I say very little about women's work and their world or the world of the child. My reason for this seemingly narrow focus on public ceremony is that it is my purpose here to demonstrate the central role of symbols and symbolic statements in the construction of cultural meanings, a key to constructing and continually recreating all the other social forms of day-to-day lived lives. In other words, it is my contention that the symbolism and rich ritual processes of the common riding have a great deal to do with experience—that is, how all these other aspects of the town are played out—and that by understanding something about how symbols do their work and how they mean, we will better understand some of the secrets of culture.

Appendix
Common Riding Day—
Sequence of Events[1]

4:00 A.M. Rouse parade: The flute band walks around the town, waking in turn the standard bearer and the provost.

5:30 A.M. An act of remembrance is made by the ex-soldiers at the war memorial.

6:00 A.M. The first drum is sounded by the silver band, which plays "Hail, Smiling Morn" around the town.

6:15 A.M. The exiles' song, "Her Bright Smile," is sung outside the County Hotel.

6:30 A.M. The foot procession arrives at Victoria Halls. Meanwhile, the riders assemble in Back Row.

6:45 A.M. The burgh standard bearer is installed, and the bussin' o' the burgh flag is held on the balcony of Victoria Hall.

6:55 A.M. The procession forms and marches to the Market Place. The order of the procession is as follows:
1. The Selkirk Silver Band.
2. The Incorporation of Hammermen.
3. The Incorporation of Weavers.
4. The Colonial Society.
5. The Selkirk Pipe Band.
6. The Ex-Servicemen's Association.
7. The Merchant Company.
8. The Burgh Officers.
9. The Councillors and Officials.

          10. The Ex–Standard Bearers.
              Mounted:
          11. The Royal Burgh Standard Bearer.
          12. The Attendants and Burleymen.
          13. The Mounted Councillors.
          14. All other mounted followers.

7:00 A.M. The second drum: The procession moves off "down the Green" to the tune "O' a'the Airts." The riders ford the River Ettrick.

7:45 A.M. The riders in the Linglie Glen: The foot procession returns to the Market Place and disperses for breakfast.

8:45 A.M. The riders at summit, Three Brethren.

9:00 A.M. The procession leaves the Market Place for Shawburn Toll to the tunes "When You and I Were Young Maggie" and "The Boys of the Old Brigade."

9:30 A.M. At the Toll: Community singing led by the bands until the "comin' in of the Burley."

10:15 A.M. The procession reforms and returns to the Market Place to the tunes "Stirling Brig" and "The Flo'ers o' the Forest."

11:00 A.M. The Casting of the Colours to the tune of "Up wi' the Souters o' Selkirk," with each standard bearer in turn performing this unique ceremony.
The order of casting flags[2] is as follows:
    1. The Royal and Ancient Burgh.
    2. The Hammermen.
    3. The Weavers.
    4. The Colonial Society.
    5. The Merchants.
    6. The Ex-Servicemen.

11:10 A.M. This is a two-minute silence and the lament for Flodden, "The Liltin'."

11:15 A.M. The burgh flag is returned "unsullied and untarnished." The national anthem is sung. The Silver Band leads the United Crafts from the Market Place; the Pipe Band leads the ex-servicemen from the Market Place. All others disperse.

2:00 P.M. The race meeting is held at the Gala Rig, along with amateur races and "flaps."

8:00 P.M. The Common Riding Ball begins.

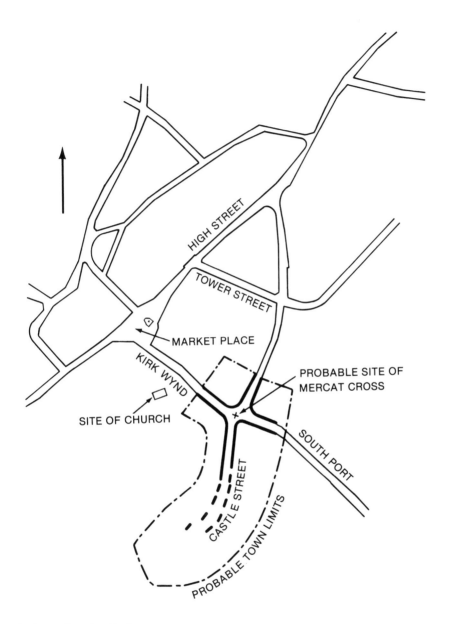

Early Medieval Selkirk in relation to the modern town center. *(Based on a map by Walter Elliot of Selkirk.)*

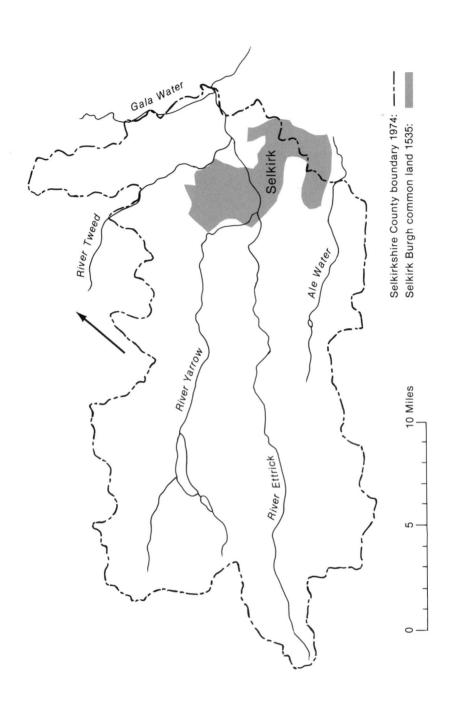

Gala Water

Selkirk

River Tweed

River Yarrow

River Ettrick

Ale Water

Selkirkshire County boundary 1974: —·——·—
Selkirk Burgh common land 1535:

0   5   10 Miles

Selkirk's common lands in 1535. (Based on a map by Jack Harper of Selkirk.)

Notes

Preface

1. The material on regions and ritual was first published in my 1979 "Community Form and Ceremonial Life in Three Regions of Scotland."

2. My interest in the town as a culture structure and a symbolic social form comes in part from my studies of urban anthropology and the early anthropology of community form pioneered by W. Lloyd Warner (1961), Conrad Arensberg and Solon Kimball (1965), and Lewis Mumford (1970). I am also indebted to the insights from Rykwert's history of archaeology and art history (1988) and to the teachings of archaeologists Charles Fairbanks and James Ford at the University of Florida.

The themes of individual and community are concerns of both Weber (1958) and Durkheim (1947). These questions of the symbolic construction of individualism and the conceptual schemes and social forms linking individual to group have continued to occupy a long line of British and European social thinkers into the present day; see, for example, Cohen 1985a and Strathern 1981. Recently the questions and problems have been posed from the social point of view in an enlightening manner in American anthropology by Peacock and Tyson in *Pilgrims of Paradox* (1989) and James Boon (1989) in *Affinities and Extremes*.

3. Among the recent framers of these questions is Clifford Geertz (1973). Also, the whole matter of ritual life as process and metaphor is built on the questions and models of Victor Turner, found early on in *The Ritual Process* (1969) and later in his works devoted to exploring these crucial themes for understanding cultural meanings and social life (1975, 1982, also Turner and Bruner 1986). Other scholars of ritual whose work parallels my own—especially those pertaining to civic ritual, festival, and the relation of secular to religious ritual arenas—include Roger Abrahams (1982), Sally Falk Moore and Barbara Myerhoff (1977), Jill Dubisch (1991), David Kertzer (1988), Michael Herzfeld (1992), Ellen Badone (1992), Alan Dundes (Dundes and Falassi 1975) and Allesandro Falassi (1987), and Edward Muir (1981). See also the work of Frank Manning (1973), Ronald Grimes (1976), Bruce Kapferer (1979), John MacAloon (1984), Richard Scheckner (1985), S. J. Tambiah (1981), and Roy Wagner (1981).

4. I am especially grateful to the speakers for the Brown Symposium at Southwestern University organized by Ellsworth Peterson, on "Benjamin Britten and the Ceremony of Innocence." I note particularly Eric Crozier for his talk on Albert Herring. See also Kerman (1956), *Opera as Drama*.

Introduction

1. For this use of the idea of sampler, I am indebted to the work of Tyson, Peacock, and Patterson (1988) on independent Protestants in North Carolina, entitled *Diversities of Gifts*.

Chapter 1

1. See Pierce 1955:263, quoted in Singer 1984:117. For a description of the return scene in Icelandic sagas, see Bauman 1986. Also see Aries 1974 for a discussion of the romantic staging of death in the *Chansons de Roland*.

2. Townsfolk deny that the figure resembles a madonna and child of Mediterranean Europe or that there is any connection to earlier images of the Virgin Mary lingering in and through the town's symbolism beyond the Reformation campaign to erase any such iconography. Elsewhere I have suggested that the town has seized on Roman Catholic symbols in its representation of its traditional life in the face of modernization and "Protestanization" (see Neville 1987b). On the association of civic festivals with sacred themes, see Ozouf 1988, and on the flag symbolism of the French, see Agulhon 1985. Also see Moore and Myerhoff 1977 on the general theme of secular ritual.

3. In connecting cognitive and symbolic worlds to economic ones I follow Weber 1958. Ariès (1974, 1982), Stannard (1974), and others have documented aspects of the process transforming death from medieval to modern thought and practice. See also Bloch and Parry 1982. The typical American popular death rituals described by various writers for an emerging secular culture are not in keeping with Protestant Reformed Christianity and are therefore seen by Presbyterian ministers and theologians on both sides of the Atlantic as evidence of popular culture creeping into the realm reserved for church observances.

Chapter 2

1. In a reference to the order of precedence of the guilds in the common riding procession, the hammermen's official history. Selkirk magistrates are said to have petitioned the authorities in Edinburgh in 1709 as to which craft by right should lead the town's processions. The answer calls on traditions going back into the early processions of royal burghs. The example given is that of Aberdeen, whose city records of 1513

reveal that they too petitioned Edinburgh in that earlier year for similar guidance, and the fact emerges in that town processions were led by a bearer carrying high above all, the consecrated Wafer on top of the Cross, and followed immediately by the Hammermen, thus signifying that Christ had been a carpenter during his earthly life. In the days of Mother Church in Scotland, all aspects pertaining to Christ's earthly life would be observed and traditions continue. So these present two possible reasons for Edinburgh's decision, in both cases two different towns at two vastly different periods. *Incorporation of Hammermen* 1981:10–11)

2. Several recent studies of initiation rituals and the cultural making of ideas of masculine adulthood deal in more elaborate detail with this theme of male brotherhoods and their symbolism. See Carnes 1989, Gilmore 1990, and Herzfeld 1985.

3. The town commons has gradually been sold off over the years until the present portion owned by the town is only a fraction of its original size. A large portion was sold to mills for manufacturing sites along the Ettrick River. The power and control of the burgesses remained tight in these enterprises and in the management of the town's lands until the Burgh Reform Act of 1833 gave wider franchise of voting. In 1975 the town councils were completely disassembled by Parliament in a government reorganization known as the "regionalization" of local governments (Smout 1969, 1986). The office of provost is now entirely ceremonial.

Chapter 3

1. I have argued elsewhere (Neville 1987a) that the mother as liturgist appears prominently in rituals of reunion in the American South, such as at family reunions, camp meetings, cemetery association days, and others. In these liminal settings, I find an inversion of cultural rules and a reversal of social roles for women. These liminal reversals can also be seen at weddings and funerals in America. The common riding is quite different in many ways, in that it is civic based rather than kin or church based. The intricate intermeshing of women's and men's roles in ritual throughout Anglo-Celtic cultural worlds remains an inviting field for further analysis.

2. Several sources have informed my analysis of the public ceremonial aspects of the common riding, in addition to those cited in the text. These include Kertzer 1988, Hayden 1987, and MacAloon 1984.

Chapter 4

1. For an excellent collection of articles on Selkirk's past, see Gilbert 1985.

2. Davies (1955) addressed issues of patriotism and war memorials, as did Warner (1961) in his treatment of civic patriotism toward Yankee City in its tercentenary celebration. I dealt with these themes in the common riding in more detail in my 1989 article, "The Sacred and the Civic: Representations of Death in the Town Ceremony of Border Scotland."

3. See Carnes's (1989) work on men's associations in Victorian America.

4. See Gluckman's *Rituals of Rebellion in South-East Africa* (1954), and Peacock's *Rites of Modernization* (1968).

5. See Warner on Yankee City in *The Family of God* (1961).

6. See Arensberg's chapter, "Peoples of the Old World," in Arensberg and Kimball, *Culture and Community* (1965).

7. On early Viking towns and the general organization of northern Europe in the eighth century and beyond, see Clarke and Ambrosiani 1991. On the construction of medieval town-ness through "acts of rule," see Fradenburg 1991. Other sources exploring towns and villages in relation to cultural, social, and economic features include the following: Abrams and Wrigley 1978, Frisch 1972, Golby 1986, Gregg 1950, Wrightson and Levine 1979, and Seebohm 1971. On symbol and meaning in the construction of Scottish and English culture, see also Chapman 1978 and Howe 1989.

Chapter 5

1. For my understanding of ceremony as performance, I am indebted to the work of several anthropologists, including Milton Singer 1980 and 1984, Richard Bauman 1977 and 1986, Erving Goffman 1967, and James Peacock 1968.

2. Some scholars, including Manning (1973) and Abrahams (1982), have used the concept of play as an analytical device for the study of festival and ritual.

3. My model for ritual analysis is a composite drawn from a number of sources, including Turner 1969, Boon 1982, and Geertz 1973; see also Moore and Myerhoff 1977.

4. I presented an earlier version of the material on religious symbolism as a paper in a session on ritual in Europe organized by Ellen Badone for the American Ethnological Society (see Neville 1987b).

Appendix

1. The text of this sequence of events is reproduced as closely as possible to the original text of a brochure printed and distributed locally in Selkirk between 1966 and 1975 by Walter Thompson. Its title is *Selkirk Common Riding*. A picture of the procession going "down the green" is found on the cover, and under the picture is the caption "Held annually on the Friday following the second Monday in June," and after another space, "The Common Riding Day—The Proceedings, Their History and Origin."

2. The Fleshers Incorporation did not cast a flag for some years, so that in this version of the order of events their name is not mentioned. In recent years this society has been revitalized as a common riding ceremonial organization and now casts its flag after the weavers.

References

Abrahams, Roger. 1982. "The Language of Festivals: Celebrating the Economy." In Victor Turner (ed.), *Celebration: Studies in Festivities and Ritual*, pp. 161–177. Washington, D.C.: Smithsonian Press.

Abrams, Philip, and E. A. Wrigley (eds.). 1978. *Towns in Societies: Essays in Economic History and Historical Sociology*. Cambridge: Cambridge University Press.

Agulhon, Maurice. 1981. *Marianne into Battle: Republican Imagery and Symbolism in France 1789–1880*. Trans. Janet Lloyd. Cambridge: Cambridge University Press.

———. 1985. "Politics, Images and Symbols in Post Revolutionary France." In Sean Wilentz (ed.), *Rites of Power*, pp. 177–205. Philadelphia: University of Pennsylvania Press.

Arensberg, C. M., and Solon Kimball. 1965. *Culture and Community*. New York: Harcourt Brace.

———. 1968 [1940]. *Family and Community in Ireland*. 2nd ed. Cambridge, Mass: Harvard University Press.

Ariès, Phillipe. 1974. *Western Attitudes Toward Death from the Middle Ages to the Present*. Baltimore: John Hopkins University Press.

———. 1982. *The Hour of Our Death*. New York: Random House.

Babcock, Barbara A. 1978. "Introduction." In Barbara A. Babcock (ed.), *The Reversible World*, pp. 13–36. Ithaca, N.Y.: Cornell University Press.

Badone, Ellen (ed.). 1992. *Religious Orthodoxy and Popular Faith in European Society*. Princeton, N.J.: Princeton University Press.

Barth, Frederick (ed.). 1969. *Ethnic Groups and Boundaries: The Social Organization of Cultural Difference*. Boston: Little, Brown.

Bauman, Richard. 1977. *Verbal Art as Performance*. Rowley, Mass.: Newberry House.

———. 1986. "Performance and Honor in 13th Century Iceland." *Journal of American Folklore* 99 (392): 131–49.

Bloch, Maurice, and Jonathan Parry (eds.). 1982. *Death and the Regeneration of Life*. Cambridge: Cambridge University Press.

Boon, James. 1982. *Other Tribes, Other Scribes: Symbolic Anthropology in the Comparative Study of Cultures, Histories, Religions, and Texts*. Cambridge: Cambridge University Press.

———. 1989. *Affinities and Extremes*. Chicago: University of Chicago Press.

Bourdieu, Pierre. 1977. *Outline of a Theory of Practice*. Trans. Richard Nice. Cambridge: Cambridge University Press.

Brengues, Jacques. 1974. "L'Apport de la franc-maçonnerie á la fête révolutionaire." *Humanism*, July–August 1974.

Brown, Ian. 1985. "The Reformed Burgh." In John M. Gilbert (ed.), *The Flower of the Forest: Selkirk, a New History*, pp. 136–147. Galashiels: Byway Books.

Cannadine, David. 1980. *Lords and Landlords: The Aristocracy and the Towns 1774–1967*. Leicester: Leicester University Press.

———. 1983. "The British Monarchy c. 1820–1077." In Eric Hobsbawm and Terrence Ranger (eds.), *The Invention of Tradition*, pp. 101–64. Cambridge: Cambridge University Press.

Carnes, Mark C. 1989. *Secret Ritual and Manhood in Victorian America*. New Haven, Conn.: Yale University Press.

Chapman, Malcolm. 1978. *The Gaelic Vision in Scottish Culture*. Montreal: McGill–Queens University Press.

Clarke, Helen, and Björn Ambrosiani. 1991. *Towns in the Viking Age*. New York: St. Martin's Press.

Cohen, Anthony P. 1985a. *The Symbolic Construction of Community*. Chichester: Ellis Horwood.

———. 1985b. "Symbolism and Social Change: Matters of Life and Death in Whalsay, Shetland." *Man* 20: 307–24.

Cotte, Roger. 1975. "Contribution to the Clermont Conference." *Annales historiques de la révolution française* 47 (221).

Davies, Wallace Evan. 1955. *Patriotism on Parade: The Story of Veteran's and Hereditary Organizations in America 1783–1900*. Cambridge, Mass: Harvard University Press.

Dubisch, Jill. 1991. *Gender and Power in Rural Greece*. Princeton, N.J.: Princeton University Press.

Dundes, Alan, and Allessandro Falassi. 1975. *La Terra in piazza*. Berkeley and Los Angeles: University of California Press.

Durkheim, Emile. 1947 [1915]. *Elementary Forms of the Religious Life*. Glencoe, Ill.: Free Press.

Eidson, John. 1990. "German Club Life as a Local Cultural System." *Comparative Studies in Society and History* 32(2): 357–82.

Falassi, Allessandro. 1987. *Time out of Time: Essays on the Festival*. Albuquerque, N.M.: University of New Mexico Press.

Fischer, Michael M. J. 1989. "Museums and Festivals: Notes on the Poetics and Politics of Representation Conference, the Smithsonian Institution. September 26–28, 1988, Ivan Carp and Steven Levine, Organisers." *Cultural Anthropology* 4(2):204–21.

Fradenburg, Louise Olga. 1991. *City, Marriage, Tournament: Arts of Rule in Late Medieval Scotland*. Madison: University of Wisconsin Press.

Frese, Pamela, and John Coggeshall (eds.). 1991. *Transcending Boundaries: Multidisciplinary Approaches to the Study of Gender*. New York: Begin and Garvey.

Frisch, Michael H. 1972. *Town into City: Springfield, Massachusetts and the Meaning of Community, 1840–1880*. Cambridge, Mass.: Harvard University Press.

Gash, Norman. 1979. *Aristocracy and People: Britain 1815–1865*. Cambridge, Mass.: Harvard University Press.

Geertz, Clifford. 1973. *The Interpretation of Cultures*. New York: Basic Books.

Gilbert, John M. (ed.). 1985. *Flower of the Forest: Selkirk, a New History*. Selkirk: Selkirk Common Good Fund.

Gilmore, David. 1990. *Manhood in the Making: Cultural Concepts of Masculinity*. New Haven, Conn.: Yale University Press.

Gluckman, Max. 1954. *Rituals of Rebellion in South-East Africa*. Manchester: Manchester University Press.

Goffman, Erving. 1967. *Interaction Ritual*. New York: Anchor Books.

Golby, I. M. (ed.). 1986. *Culture and Society in Britain 1850–1890: A Sourcebook of Contemporary Writings*. Oxford: Oxford University Press in association with Open University.

Gregg, Pauline. 1950. *A Social and Economic History of Britain 1760–1972*. London: Harrap.

Grimes, R. 1976. *Symbol and Conquest: Public Ritual and Drama in Santa Fe*. Ithaca, N.Y.: Cornell University Press.

Gulvin, Clifford. 1973. *The Tweedmakers: A History of the Scottish Fancy Woolen Industry, 1600–1914*. Newton Abbott: David & Charles; New York: Barnes & Noble.

Harper, Jack. 1985. *The Common, the Flag, and the Song*. Selkirk: Walter Thompson.

Hayden, Ilse. 1987. *Symbol and Privilege: The Ritual Context of British Royalty*. Tucson: University of Arizona Press.

Herzfeld, Michael. 1985. *The Poetics of Manhood*. Princeton, N.J.: Princeton University Press.

———. 1992. *A Place in History*. Princeton, N.J.: Princeton University Press.

Hobsbawm, Eric. 1983. "Introduction: Inventing Traditions." In Eric Hobsbawm and Terrance Ranger (eds.), *The Invention of Tradition*, pp. 263–307. Cambridge: Cambridge University Press.

Howe, Nicholas. 1989. *Migration and Mythmaking in Anglo-Saxon England*. New Haven, Conn.: Yale University Press.

Huntington, Richard, and Peter Metcalf. 1979. *Celebrations of Death: The Anthropology of Mortuary Ritual*. Cambridge: Cambridge University Press.

Incorporation of Hammermen, Selkirk. 1981. *The History of the Selkirk Hammermen*. Selkirk: Walter Thompson.

Kapferer, Bruce. 1979. "Introduction: Ritul Process and the Transformation of Context." *Social Analysis* 1:3–19.

Kerman, Joseph. 1956. *Opera as Drama*. New York: Knopf.

Kertzer, David. 1988. *Ritual, Politics, and Power*. New Haven, Conn.: Yale University Press.

Leach, Edmund. 1954. *Political Systems of Highland Burma*. London: G. Bell and Sons.

Leach, E. R. 1976. *Culture and Communication: The Logic by Which Symbols Are Connected*. Cambridge: Cambridge University Press.

Lévi-Strauss, Claude. 1963. *Structural Anthropology*. New York: Basic Books.

MacAloon, John J. (ed.). 1984. *Rite, Drama, Festival, Spectacle: Rehearsals Toward a Theory of Cultural Performance*. Philadelphia: Institute for the Study of Human Issues.

Manning, Frank. 1973. *Black Clubs in Bermuda: Ethnography of a Play World*. Ithaca, N.Y.: Cornell University Press.

Mauss, Marcel. 1967. *The Gift*. Trans. I. Cunnison. New York: Norton.

Metzger, Lore. 1986. *One Foot in Eden: Modes of Pastoral in Romantic Poetry*. Chapel Hill: University of North Carolina Press.

Mingay, G. E. 1963. *English Landed Society in the Eighteenth Century*. London: Routledge & Kegan Paul.

Moore, G. Alexander. 1980. "Walt Disney World: Bounded Ritual Space and the Playful Pilgrimage Center." *Anthropological Quarterly* 53 (4):207–18.

Moore, Sally F., and Barbara Myerhoff. 1977. "Introduction: Secular Ritual—Forms and Meanings." In Sally F. Moore and Barbara Myerhoff (eds.), *Secular Ritual*, pp. 3–24. Amsterdam: Van Gorcum.

Moorhouse, Geoffrey. 1992. *Hell's Foundations: A Social History of the Town of Bury in the Aftermath of the Gallipoli Campaign*. New York: Henry Holt.

Muir, Edward. 1981. *Civic Ritual in Renaissance Venice*. Princeton, N.J.: Princeton University Press.

Mumford, Lewis. 1970 [1938]. *The Culture of Cities*. New York: Harcourt Brace Jovanovich.

Myerhoff, Barbara. 1978. *Number Our Days*. New York: Simon & Schuster.

Neville, Gwen Kennedy. 1974. "Kinfolks and the Covenant: Ethnic Community Among Southern Presbyterians." In John Bennett (ed.), *The New Ethnicity: Perspectives from Ethnology*. Proceedings of the annual spring meeting, American Ethnological Society, pp. 258–74. Chicago: West.

———. 1979. "Community Form and Ceremonial Life in Three Regions of Scotland." *American Ethnologist* 6(1):93–109.

———. 1986. "Civic Ceremony as Performance, Ritual and Play: Common Riding in the Scottish Borders." Paper presented to the eighty-fifth annual meeting of the American Anthropological Association, Philadelphia.

———. 1987a. *Kinship and Pilgrimage: Rituals of Reunion in American Protestant Culture*. New York: Oxford University Press.

————. 1987b. "Religious Symbols and Secular Ritual: Common Riding and the Construction of Culture in the Scottish Borders." Paper presented to the annual meeting of the American Ethnological Society, San Antonio.

————. 1989. "The Sacred and the Civic: Representations of Death in the Town Ceremony of Border Scotland." *Anthropology Quarterly* 62(4):163–74.

Ortner, Sherry. 1978. *Sherpas Through Their Rituals*. Cambridge: Cambridge University Press.

Ozouf, Mona. 1988. *Festivals and the French Revolution*. Cambridge, Mass.: Harvard University Press.

Peacock, James. 1968. *Rites of Modernization*. Chicago: University of Chicago Press.

————. 1975. *Consciousness and Change: Symbolic Anthropology in Evolutionary Perspective*. New York: Wiley.

Peacock, James, and Ruel Tyson, Jr. 1989. *Pilgrims of Paradox*. Washington, D.C.: Smithsonian Press.

Pierce, C. S. 1955. *Philosophical Writings of Pierce*. Ed. J. Buchler. New York: Dover.

Rearick, Charles. 1977. "Festivals in Modern France: The Experience of the 3rd Republic." *Journal of Contemporary History* 12 (3):435–60.

Roberts, Stewart. 1985a. "The Textile Industry." In John M. Gilbert (ed.), *Flower of the Forest: Selkirk, a New History*. pp. 106–119. Galashiels: Byway Books.

————. 1985b. "Selkirk in the Twentieth Century." In John M. Gilbert (ed.), *Flower of the Forest: Selkirk, a New History*. Galashiels: Byway Books.

Rykwert, Joseph. 1988 [1976]. *The Idea of a Town*. Cambridge, Mass.: MIT Press.

Sahlins, Marshall. 1976. *Culture and Practical Reason*. Chicago: University of Chicago Press.

Sales, Roger. 1983. *English Literature in History 1780–1830: Pastoral and Politics*. New York: St. Martin's Press.

Scheckner, Richard. 1985. *Between Theater and Anthropology*. Philadelphia: University of Pennsylvania Press.

Schmidt, Leigh Eric. 1989. *Holy Fairs: Scottish Communions and American Revivals in the Early Modern Period*. Princeton, N.J.: Princeton University Press.

Schneider, David. 1976. "Notes Toward a Theory of Culture." In Keith Basso and Henry Selby (eds.), *Meaning in Anthropology*, pp. 197–220. Albuquerque: University of New Mexico Press.

Seebohm, Fredrick. 1971 [1883]. *The English Village Community*. Port Washington, N.Y.: Kennikat Press.

Simmel, George. 1950. *The Sociology of George Simmel*. Ed. and trans. Kurt N. Wolf. New York: Free Press.

Singer, Milton. 1980 [1972]. *When a Great Tradition Modernizes*. Chicago: University of Chicago Press.

———. 1984. *Man's Glassy Essence*. Bloomington: Indiana University Press.

Smout, T. C. 1969. *A History of the Scottish People 1560–1830*. London: Collins/Fontana.

———. 1970. "The Landowner and the Planned Village." In N. T. Phillipson and Rosalind Mitchison (eds.), *Scotland in the Age of Improvement: Essays in Scottish History in the Eighteenth Century*, pp. 73–106. Edinburgh: University of Edinburgh Press.

———. 1986. *A Century of the Scottish People 1830-1950*. New Haven, Conn.: Yale University Press.

Stannard, David E. (ed.). 1974. *Death in America*. Philadelphia: University of Pennsylvania Press.

Strathern, Marilyn. 1981. *Kinship at the Core*. Cambridge: Cambridge University Press.

Tambiah, S. J. 1981. "A Performance Approach to Ritual" (Radcliffe-Brown Lecture, 1979). *Proceedings of the British Academy* 65:113–69.

Turner, Victor. 1969. *The Ritual Process*. Chicago: Aldine.

———. 1975. *Dramas, Fields, and Metaphors: Symbolic Action in Human Society*. Ithaca, N.Y.: Cornell University Press.

Turner, Victor, and E. M. Bruner (eds.). 1986. *The Anthropology of Experience*. Urbana: University of Illinois Press.

Turner, Victor, and Edith Turner. 1978. *Image and Pilgrimage in Christian Culture*. New York: Columbia University Press.

Tyson, Ruel, Jr., James Peacock, and Daniel Patterson (eds.). 1988. *Diversities of Gifts*. Urbana: University of Illinois Press.

Wagner, Roy. 1981. *The Invention of Culture*. 2nd ed. Chicago: University of Chicago Press.

Warner, W. Lloyd. 1961. *The Family of God: A Symbolic Study of Christian Life in America*. New Haven, Conn.: Yale University Press.

Weber, Max. 1958 [1905]. *The Protestant Ethic and the Spirit of Capitalism*. Trans. Talcott Parsons. New York: Scribner.

Williams, Raymond. 1973. *The Country and the City*. New York: Oxford University Press.

Wolf, Eric. 1982. *Europe and the People Without History*. Berkeley and Los Angeles: University of California Press.

Wrightson, Keith, and David Levine. 1979. *Poverty and Piety in an English Village: Terling 1525–1700*. New York: Academic Press.

Index

DATE DUE